The Corona Crash

The Corona Crash

How the Pandemic Will Change Capitalism

Grace Blakeley

VERSO

London • New York

First published by Verso 2020
© Grace Blakeley 2020

The moral rights of the author have been asserted

1 3 5 7 9 10 8 6 4 2

Verso
UK: 6 Meard Street, London W1F 0EG
US: 20 Jay Street, Suite 1010, Brooklyn, NY 11201
versobooks.com

Verso is the imprint of New Left Books

ISBN-13: 978-1-83976-205-5
ISBN-13: 978-1-83976-206-2 (UK EBK)
ISBN-13: 978-1-83976-207-9 (US EBK)

British Library Cataloguing in Publication Data
A catalogue record for this book is
available from the British Library

Library of Congress Cataloging-in-Publication Data
A catalog record for this book is available
from the Library of Congress

Typeset in Sabon MT by Hewer Text UK Ltd, Edinburgh
Printed and bound by CPI Group (UK) Ltd, Croydon CR0 4YY

Contents

Preface

Few could have imagined that 2020 would be the year the world entered a new phase of capitalism, as the links between states, banks and the world's biggest corporations become so tight that they seem to fuse entirely. The stagnation of the past decade represented the death knell of the speculative mania that characterised the era of financialisation, which collapsed under the weight of its own excesses in 2008. Amid the pandemic, we have witnessed its replacement – state monopoly capitalism – begin to emerge.

Within weeks of the declaration of a pandemic by the World Health Organisation on 11 March, it became clear that the public health emergency would cause widespread economic devastation. There were three quarters of a million confirmed cases of Covid-19 by the end of March and the constraints on ordinary economic activity imposed in response to its spread had brought the global economy to a standstill.

The Great Lockdown – as the coordinated stay-at-home and social-distancing measures imposed by many states around the world have been termed – had an immediate impact on the labour market, output, incomes and consumption. Stock markets plummeted more than during any other recent crisis. The S&P and the Dow Jones saw some of their largest one-day falls in history. Falling stock prices reflected investors' realisation that, with factories closed, borders shut and consumption and investment both collapsing, the global economy was headed into a deep recession. After a decade of rising corporate debt, the big worry was that falling corporate incomes would cause a cascade of corporate bankruptcies that could threaten some major financial institutions.

But despite all this, by June the Great Lockdown was being eased, stock markets had recovered most of their losses and commentators began once again to talk up the likelihood of a V-shaped recovery. There is always a point in the middle of a crisis when people convince themselves that the worst is over – call it the eye of the storm. The FTSE 100 rallied in the immediate aftermath of the run on Northern Rock in 2007, even though it was obvious by that point that many other banks were just as vulnerable to a deterioration in credit conditions. After the first wave of the Spanish flu in 1918, people convinced themselves that the worst was over, only to be hit with another, more severe wave just a few months later.[1]

It seems clear that, at the time of this writing, the global economy is in the eye of the Covid-19 storm. Deaths around the world continue to mount, and while many countries are managing safely to reopen their economies by stepping up testing and tracing measures, others are ending lockdown without any plans whatsoever. Until a vaccine is found, we cannot dismiss the possibility that the world will face further waves of the virus that will require a recommencement of lock-down measures.

What's more, the virus is now spreading to new parts of the global economy. As Kim Moody pointed out in an essay for the journal *Spectre*,[2] the coronavirus initially spread through the veins and arteries of the world's trade system: it began in Wuhan, a global centre of commodity production, before making its way through commercial hubs in East Asia, commodities exporters in the Middle East and Latin America, and the centres of global consumption in Europe and North America.

From London, Washington and New York, the virus spread to the hinterlands of the economies of the imperial core, leading to new outbreaks in the Midlands of the UK and the southern states of the US. And while initially protected due to its peripheral position in the world capitalist system, sub-Saharan Africa is now seeing an increase in cases, emanating from trading centres in Nigeria and South Africa. Public health experts have long been warning of the catastrophic impact the virus could have if it begins to spread quickly in the poorest countries in the Global South. Many of these states are already suffering from deep debt distress, with governments being forced to choose between servicing their obligations to creditors and purchasing ventilators and protective equipment for medical staff.

But it is not just in the Global South that the pre-existing weaknesses created by uneven, financialised capitalist development are about to be exacerbated by the pandemic. So far, debt-laden economies in the Global North like the US, the UK and Ireland have managed to avoid a financial crisis as a result of the pandemic – but a senior official at the Federal Reserve has warned that looming bankruptcies could still trigger one.[3]

Governments have stepped in to defer consumer loan and credit card payments, act as guarantor for bank lending to small businesses, and pump almost unlimited liquidity into their domestic corporate sectors, which were already over-leveraged before the pandemic struck. But each of these measures rests on the assumption that firms and households will ultimately be able to repay the loans. If the problem is simply that consumers and businesses are struggling to access cash, then this would be the sensible option. But if we are headed for a depression in which many of them will barely be able to cover their bottom lines, let alone repay all their debts, then all the new lending in the world won't make a difference.

The fact that banks coordinating the government's 'bounceback loan' scheme in the UK have already stated that between 40 to 50 per cent of the small businesses receiving these loans will default when the scheme ends warns of trouble to come.[4] Moreover, the central assumption of the Office for Budget Responsibility – echoed by international institutions like the IMF – is that unemployment will climb to 12 per cent and remain in double figures well into 2021.[5] In the US, some economists are projecting that it will reach at least 15 per cent.[6]

How will struggling businesses and unemployed consumers be able to honour their obligations to creditors if they aren't earning? And if they don't honour their obligations, who will pick up the slack? Will the state write off loans and force the banks that issued the debt to take a hit? Or will the pain be forced onto workers and small and medium-sized businesses, while investors in the corporate sector remain hooked up to government life support in perpetuity?

We have no answers to any of these questions, and the fact that the governments of the US and the UK seem to be making things up as they go along does not make it any easier to guess. In the context of this dramatic – almost unprecedented – uncertainty, the optimism of the summer months of 2020 is, at some point, likely to give way to a self-reinforcing cycle of pessimism. Although much depends on the policy response, societies around the world are facing mass unemployment, falling incomes and widespread corporate and personal defaults. Far from a V-shaped recession, it will probably take years for the economy to recover to pre-crisis output levels. The UK's services-dependent economy is expected to be the worst hit within the OECD.[7]

The severity of the pandemic-induced recession is at least in part a result of the pre-existing vulnerabilities of the global economy. After a decade of slow growth, surging debt levels and rising inequality, we can rarely have been worse prepared for a new recession. The recovery from the 2008 financial crisis was characterised, above all, by stagnation – of wages, productivity and investment. Many wealthy economies saw the share of national income taken by labour fall.[8] For the first time in decades, globalisation had gone into 'retreat', owing to the difficulties of its financial wing. Cross-border capital flows declined by 65 per cent between 2007 and 2016.[9] Global growth was buoyed only by incredibly cheap credit and public investment under-taken by developmental states in the Global South. Central bankers were forced to keep the economy on life support through ultra-low interest rates and quan-titative easing. But even with monetary policy so loose, private investment in fixed capital was not forthcom-ing. Instead, the main effect of low interest rates was to inflate a debt bubble three times the size of global GDP.[10]

The problem was clear: capitalism had lost all momentum. Many economists were predicting that a recession would hit the US, the UK and the Eurozone by 2022.[11] The yield curve, which shows the returns on US Treasuries of different maturities, had inverted for the first time since 2007 – meaning that short-term govern-ment bonds had higher yields than long-term bonds.[12] An inverted yield curve has augured every major reces-sion for the last half century. In the end, the recession came earlier – and hit unimaginably harder – than expected.

All over the world, capitalists were already look-ing to nation-states to save them from the overlapping crises of secular stagnation, populism and climate breakdown. The Covid-19 recession has strengthened demands for government intervention, while further weakening profits and increasing the dependence of capital on the state. Central bankers and politicians have staged unprecedented economic interventions, not to help the most vulnerable through this crisis, but to save capitalism from itself. The beneficiaries will be big business, big banks and powerful political interests.

As the coronavirus unfolds in the UK, the Right is in power, and they are demanding that journalists, citizens and even health officials fall in line behind the government narrative. Questioning government policy – whether on monetary policy, statutory sick pay or welfare payments – is 'politicising' a public health crisis. The idea that the coronavirus crisis can be 'politicised' is to imply that it is not already an inherently political event. Of course, the outbreak of the virus was a natural event – though one that seems to have been prompted by unsustainable farming practices undertaken in the name of profit maximisation.[13] But its economic impact, and, in particular, the distribution of costs, could not be more political. And governments are working hard to ensure that the costs do not fall on the wealthy and powerful.

In the US, Congress passed a $2 trillion stimulus package including loans to businesses that face a huge loss of revenue, while the Federal Reserve effectively moved to a policy of 'QE infinity'.[14] In other words, the Fed will not stop purchasing assets (using newly created central bank money) until it is satisfied that the risk to financial markets has passed. There is also an alphabet soup of asset purchasing and liquidity programmes supporting other markets. Through the CPFF, PMCCF and SMCCF, as well as the TALF, PDCF and MLF, the Fed is backstopping the market for corporate debt – paying little attention to firms' creditworthiness and absolutely no attention to their environmental impact or record on workers' rights – and the market for mortgages, auto loans, student loans and municipal bonds.[15]

More important than understanding the details of each of these programmes (which are truly vast) is understanding what they signify: the government is demonstrating its willingness to backstop the debts of US consumers, firms and states in order to prevent insolvencies and place a floor beneath falling asset prices. On the one hand, this seems like a positive short-term measure – few would argue that the Fed should simply allow personal, corporate, state and municipal bankruptcies to soar. But it also reveals something profound about the nature of modern capitalism. While there will be more business failures to come, particularly in vulnerable sectors such as high-street retail, the state is signalling to the corporate world at large that no matter how much debt it accrues during the upswing – and no matter what purposes it uses this debt for – when the crisis comes, it will be bailed out.

The implications of this message – which is also being sent by many other central banks around the world – are profound. The risks of running an investment-grade business have been socialised, while the gains have remained private. 'We are all government-sponsored enterprises now', observes Scott Minerd of Guggenheim Investments.[16] Investors are protected while the public pays the price. Over the long run, QE infinity will simply push up asset prices – including house prices – exacerbating wealth inequality. The realisation that central banks are willing to do almost anything to backstop their domestic corporate sectors and protect private wealth is a big part of what drove the stock market rallies seen through April and May 2020.

The Bank of England, the Bank of Japan and the European Central Bank have all scaled up their own asset purchasing programmes, expanding both the size of the programmes and the range of assets they are prepared to buy. These central banks are also relying on the ongoing provision of dollar liquidity through the Federal Reserve's swap line network, which has become all the more important given the dramatic expansion in dollar-denominated loans held by nonbank institutions outside the US, now thought to be worth around 14 per cent of global GDP.[17]

The trillions of dollars' worth of loans, grants and guarantees that have been generated by central banks and treasuries, in an unprecedented show of public policy firepower, quelled some of the panic in financial markets, but they have not solved the problem. In fact, piling new debt on top of old, unpayable debts will simply defer the inevitable reckoning for another day.

The general tendency across most markets will be towards consolidation, as smaller, weaker businesses fold under the pressure, or are swallowed up by their larger rivals. Some corporations will not only withstand but even gain from this crisis. Many of the world's largest businesses were sitting on huge cash piles before the pandemic hit, providing them with the

cushion they need to weather a period of falling revenues. Others – Amazon, Netflix and some of the social
media giants – actively profited from the increased
demand for their services in response to the lockdown.

What follows is a preliminary attempt to understand the political economy of the pandemic; I hope
to return to these themes more fully in due course.
We urgently need to understand the likely impact this
crisis will have on our economy and prepare accord-
ingly. The rise in state spending currently taking place
across the Global North will not usher in a socialist
nirvana. Instead, as Robert Brenner writes, policymakers have concluded 'that the only way that they can
assure the reproduction of the non-financial and financial corporations, their top managers and shareholders
– and indeed top leaders of the major parties, closely
connected with them – is to intervene politically in the
asset markets and throughout the whole economy, so
as to underwrite the upward re-distribution of wealth
to them by directly political means.'[18] The legacy of
the corona crash will be the concentration of economic
and political power in the hands of a tiny oligarchy,
composed of senior politicians, central bankers, financiers and corporate executives in the rich world.

The challenge we will face when this crisis subsides
will be to wrest control back from those who have
taken advantage of this moment to increase their power
and wealth. The only way to do so will be through a
radical democratisation of national and international
economic and political institutions, giving workers,
consumers and communities a say in decision-making

within publicly owned companies, central banks and throughout local government and the central state – and giving the poorest states in the world a voice in international governance. The alternative is to watch as democracy is finally consumed by capitalism.

1

The Last Days of
Finance Capitalism

We were still living in the shadow of the last crisis –
and the response to it – when the pandemic hit. The
US recovery from 2008 had been highly unstable and
unequal, with loose monetary policy required to sustain
unremarkable growth rates, which varied by almost 5
percentage points between the best- and worst-perform-
ing states.[1] Real average wages in the US in 2018 had the
same purchasing power as 40 years earlier.[2] Meanwhile,
corporate debt reached a record level of 75 per cent of
GDP – higher than during both the dot-com bubble of
2000 and the housing bubble of 2007.[3]

In the UK, growth had averaged less than 2 per cent
per year. This poor performance was not expected to
improve – before the pandemic sent the country into a
recession, the Bank of England forecast average annual
growth of just 1.4 per cent through to 2023.[4] There was
a chronic shortage of private investment. Gross fixed
capital formation – including fixed investment by both
the public and private sectors – stood at just 17 per cent
in 2018, compared with 21 per cent in Germany and

the United States. The UK also had a persistent current account deficit, worth 4 per cent of GDP in 2018.[5]

Mainstream economists advanced many different explanations for this economic malaise, which was reflected across many other 'advanced' economies. Some attributed it to a slowdown in technological change under the mantle of 'secular stagnation', others to rising public debt, and others to growing protectionism.[6] But the problem with mainstream explanations for the economic stagnation witnessed over the last ten years is that they only identify the symptoms of the disease, rather than the underlying cause. Most economists have been unable to determine why there has been a sudden slowdown in productivity growth, a sudden increase in government debt, and a slowdown in globalisation. They are equally at a loss to explain why all of these trends have manifested themselves at roughly the same time.

Economists failed to diagnose the root cause of the post-2008 stagnation for the same reason they failed to see the financial crisis coming in the first place. They have an incoherent account of how capitalism generates value, and their models are not built to account for broad structural shifts in political and economic institutions of the kind seen over the last forty years. The root cause of the crisis of modern capitalism does not result from a purely economic shift, but a deep-seated and long-standing transformation in political economy, the institutional foundations of which were laid in the 1980s, when the financialisation of the economy began in earnest. This trend – financialisation – is what underlay both the financial crisis and the stagnation witnessed since the crash.[7]

Finance represents a mode of accumulation distinct from other modes such as industry or commerce. Rather than using their capital to produce or trade goods or services, financiers create and trade financial assets – even if these assets are ultimately based on production that takes place elsewhere in the global economy. These assets generally take the form of a promise to pay back an amount of capital at some point in the future: for example, a share represents a claim on the future earnings of a business. The main financial activities are therefore lending, investment and speculation, and the three are often very closely intertwined. Financialisation is a process in which the logic of finance – that is, of lending, speculation and investment – penetrates all areas of economic activity to the benefit of a small financial elite and the detriment of working people. Beginning in the 1980s, financialisation became such a prominent feature of the global economy that it could be said to have defined an entire era of economic history – the era of finance-led growth.

The most obvious indicator of financialisation in the UK was the dramatic increase in the size of the finance sector itself. The UK's finance sector grew 1.5 per cent faster than the economy as a whole between 1970 and 2007 – the profits of the sector grew even faster and accounted for 15 per cent of total economy profits by 2007.[8] The output of the finance sector itself was, however, dwarfed by the growth in the assets it held. By 2007, the value of assets held by UK banks was five times the size of the British economy.[9] A significant portion of the revenues generated by the finance sector resulted from its symbiotic relationship with the real estate and insurance industries – these sectors combine to create what Michael Hudson calls the 'FIRE sectors'.[10] What they all have in common is that their profits rely on the extraction of economic rents – simple transfers of output from non-owners to owners – rather than productive economic activity that creates new value.

In his *General Theory* (1936), Keynes famously called for the 'euthanasia' of the 'functionless rentier' who made his money by charging productive capitalists for the use of scarce assets like land.[11] It is easy to believe that the problems with the British economy can be traced back to bankers who have created a warped version of capitalism that benefits a tiny elite at the expense of workers and responsible businesses. The financial crisis can be viewed as the triumph of the 'takers' over the 'makers', and the only possible solution a return to a time when our economy focused on industry, not finance and real estate.

Financialised capitalism may be a uniquely extractive way of organising the economy, but this is not to say that it represents the perversion of an otherwise sound model. Rather, it is a process that has been driven by the logic of capitalism itself. As capitalist economies develop, profits naturally increase faster than wages, inequality rises and large pools of capital accumulate in the hands of a small number of wealthy people. Meanwhile, production comes to take place at an ever-larger scale, so that productive capitalists come to rely much more heavily on external financing from banks and investors.[12] Financial institutions emerge both to provide this finance and to manage the profits that result – whether by supporting capitalists to reinvest these profits in production, or to use them for speculation or unproductive investment. As these pools of capital grow larger, financiers become more powerful – particularly the bankers able to create new money through their lending and the investors able to use the capital they manage to mediate ownership – and their interests come to merge with those of other economic actors. In this way, financialisation is a process that has come to affect each of the constituent parts of the modern economy – households, corporations and the state.

The financialisation of the modern corporation is defined by the supremacy of the ideology of shareholder value.[13] Since the 1980s, share ownership has become increasingly concentrated in the hands of institutional investors like hedge funds and pension funds. As this process intensified, incentives were created for corporate executives to distribute money to shareholders today, before investing in ways to boost the profitability of the enterprise tomorrow. In fact, nonfinancial corporations were increasingly engaging in financial activities themselves in order to secure the highest possible returns.

Under financial capitalism, financial institutions are more likely to own businesses, and businesses are more likely to invest in financial markets. Meanwhile, financiers provide the capital that big businesses need to buy up their smaller rivals – the successive waves of mergers and acquisitions activity that have taken place since the 1980s have led to dramatic increases in market concentration in many sectors, benefiting big businesses headquartered in the Global North.[14] The fact that this model is unsustainable – resting as it does on rising leverage, market concentration and short-termism – is beside the point. Production is not the point of the capitalist enterprise – profit is. And the financialisation of nonfinancial corporations has been an excellent way to maximise profit.

As the incentives to distribute ever more cash to shareholders mounted, workers' demands for their fair share of the profits were met with growing hostility. In the 1970s and 80s, rising international competition, stagflation and the decimation of the trade union movement were all used as convenient excuses for wage repression in many parts of the Global North. The inequality generated by this process presented a problem – lower wages meant falling demand, which would ultimately have constrained profitability.[15] Yet the period since the 1980s has seen an unprecedented boom in consumerism.[16] This increase in spending was largely financed not through rising real wages, but through debt.

The dramatic increases in consumer lending between 1979 and 2007 improved people's sense of prosperity and allowed them to purchase luxuries like cars, iPhones and laptops produced by hyper-exploited labour in the Global South. Some of this debt was used to purchase assets like houses, the prices of which rose as more people were able to purchase them.[17] Large sections of society in many Global North states, and a majority of the electorate, materially benefited from the new economic model through the capital gains they derived from rising asset prices. This class of 'mini-capitalists' had a material interest in the continuation of the model of debt-driven asset price inflation. The privatisation of pensions was another critical extension of this model. Together, 'property-owning democracy' and 'pension fund capitalism' sustained a bargain between financial capital and the middle classes that lasted all the way up to 2008, and is only now beginning to show signs of strain.[18]

Government itself had also become financialised. In the UK, under the private financing initiatives (PFIs) of the 1990s, government construction schemes were outsourced to private firms, which would also come up with the capital to fund the project, with the government paying them back over several decades. PFI was just one way of replacing public money with private: the privatisation of pensions schemes, the marketisation of higher education, and the privatisation of our health services have all taken liabilities off the public books and placed them with private investors. The austerity regime implemented in the wake of the 2008 financial crisis simply represented a deepening of this regime of 'privatised Keynesianism'.[19]

States used private financing to demonstrate their fiscal rectitude. Part of the reason governments considered such a demonstration necessary is that they needed private investors to believe that they will honour their debts. Demand for government debt is inversely correlated with yield: the higher the demand, the lower the interest payments. This gives the markets power to discipline states that fail to demonstrate a commitment to creditworthiness. States that fail to implement neoliberal policies can be punished through bond selloffs and runs on their currencies, giving international investors significant power to influence democratically elected governments.[20] It doesn't matter that forcing states to implement neoliberal economic policy actually reduces their creditworthiness over the long term; the time horizons of financial capitalism are shorter than at any other period in history.

The financialisation of wealthy economies in the Global North was part of a much wider process of financial globalisation. While this trend has manifested itself in the growth of the immaterial economy in the Global North, the profits that drove it were derived from the hyper-exploitation of commodity producers in the Global South.[21] Facing rising input costs and increasingly militant workers in the rich world, capitalists took advantage of falling transport costs in the 1970s and 1980s to offshore production to peripheral spaces of global capitalism. In some places, such as China, this offshoring supported the development of a domestic capitalist class and a fundamental transformation in economic relations. In others, the process merely entailed greater levels of extraction by capitalists in the Global North. Many newly independent states in the Global South didn't have the power to boost domestic industry as the Chinese state did, so foreign direct investment was focused on multinationals extracting commodities from these countries, and surplus value from their workers, while reshoring the profits to the

Global North, paying off domestic capitalists and functionaries for the privilege. The profits from production undertaken in the imperial periphery were sucked into asset markets in the global North – often via tax havens – supporting the process of financialisation and deepening inequalities between global North and South.[22]

The finance-led growth regime that has emerged over the course of the last forty years is not the first unique mode of accumulation in the history of capitalism. The one it replaced has variously been called the post-war, social democratic, or Keynesian consensus.[23] Under this growth model – underpinned by an increase in the power of labour relative to capital that emerged from the Second World War and the institutionalisation of this political settlement both domestically through the rise of state planning and internationally with the creation of the Bretton Woods institutions – the state committed itself to promoting full employment through public spending. This commitment bolstered the power of organised labour, which developed a corporatist relationship with the nation-state. The system of capital controls and exchange rate pegging agreed upon at the 1944 Bretton Woods conference supported the development of social democracy in the West and facilitated the emergence of a unique period of high growth, low unemployment and falling inequality.

Yet almost as soon as it had been implemented, the contradictions of the post-war consensus began to emerge. Controls on capital mobility were undermined by the emergence of the unregulated eurodollar markets in the City of London.[24] With the world's largest super-power facing new industrial competition abroad and an increasingly expensive war in Vietnam, Nixon in 1971 announced the end of the dollar's convertibility to gold. Two years later the oil price spike sent inflation soaring and the distributional conflict between capital and labour broke into the open across the Western world.

The collapse of the exchange rate pegging system developed at Bretton Woods and a decade of near-constant industrial conflict, economic stagnation and political turmoil created space for certain actors – namely, neoliberal academics and politicians – to consolidate support for an alternative growth model, under the watchful eye of their supporters in international finance.

Nowhere was this clearer than in the UK. Right-wing thinkers who had spent years attempting to undermine the wave of 'Marxist or Keynesian planning sweeping the globe' latched on to Margaret Thatcher's candidacy to implement their extreme free-market agenda.[25] Thatcher removed restrictions on capital mobility and deregulated banks and financial markets, leading to a near-unprecedented boom in the City. She privatised state industries, cut taxes and went to war with the UK's union movement.

Thatcher portrayed her fight against the unions as part of a strategy to 'modernise' the UK economy by weaning it off dirty, unsafe industries like coal and steel and refocusing economic activity on finance and professional services. Ultimately, the expansion of the finance sector created a self-reinforcing cycle that led to a long-term trend of deindustrialisation in the UK's regions. Capital flows into UK finance and North Sea oil drove up the value of sterling, making it even harder for the UK's manufacturers to compete internationally.[26] In 1970, financial and insurance activities made up 5 per cent of total gross value added, compared with 27 per cent for the manufacturing sector; by 2007, manufacturing and finance both made up about 10 per cent of the UK economy.[27] Most of these manufacturing jobs did not disappear – they were exported to the rest of the world. The UK became an internationalised and financialised economy, with a significant professional-managerial class whose high wages were premised upon hyper-exploitation lower down the global value chain.[28] Today, the British economy is more dependent upon the services sector than any other G7 economy.[29]

The bulk of the lower middle and working classes did not, however, immediately stand to benefit from Thatcher's transformation of the economy. As the state replaced the targeting of full employment with the targeting of inflation as the aim of macroeconomic policy, and as anti-union legislation accompanied the precaritisation of work, the power of workers declined drastically relative to their bosses. With low wages and a small state, households came to rely on dissaving and credit to fund their consumption – and businesses relied on this credit-fuelled consumption for their returns. Privatised Keynesianism effectively witnessed the substitution of public spending by debt-fuelled consumption.[30]

Those employed in clerical positions in the public and private sectors, in low-paid services like retail, hospitality and logistics and in what remained of the UK's manufacturing sector still comprised the bulk of employment.[31] Thatcher secured their support by providing the highest-paid among them with access to asset-ownership – particularly housing and private pensions.[32] The lifting of credit controls and the demutualisation of the building societies facilitated a substantial increase in mortgage lending at the same time as right-to-buy – still the largest privatisation ever undertaken by the British state – allowed social tenants to buy their houses at discounted rates.[33] With more and more credit being directed into housing, and few new houses being built, house prices soared.

British real estate was transformed from a useful commodity into a highly valuable financial asset, with ordinary working-class families benefiting from vast capital gains.[34] By 2017, UK house prices were almost ten times what they had been in 1979, next to a five-fold increase for consumer prices. Many homeowners released the equity from their properties to finance new asset purchases, or even day-to-day consumption. Household debt in Britain – primarily composed of mortgage lending – reached 148 per cent of disposable incomes in 2008, the highest it has ever been.[35]

Just as in the US, British banks took these mortgages and packed them up into financial securities, which could be sold on international capital markets, allowing them to make more loans. High levels of bank lending increased the broad money supply, and all this new money led to sharp rises in asset prices.[36] The FTSE 100 Index climbed from 1,000 points in 1984 to over 6,000 in 1999, dipping for a time before returning to this level in 2006–07.[37] The new financial securities created by British banks were bought up by investors all over the world. Rising asset prices attracted yet more international capital, creating a self-reinforcing cycle that led many to believe that the party would continue forever. But ultimately this model, like any premised on the continuous expansion of private credit, proved unsustainable. The combination of capital mobility and financial deregulation had led to the emergence of a huge speculative bubble that would eventually pop.

When the US government decided on 12 September 2008 to allow Lehman Brothers to fail, the decision sent financial markets into free fall. In Britain, the accumulation strategies developed by the finance sector – including securitisation, derivatives trading and foreign exchange speculation – lay in tatters as international banking seized up and global capital flows ceased. The coterie of consultants, accountants and lawyers dependent upon the City of London suffered from the loss of demand from both domestic and international clients. The real estate sector was, of course, initially completely paralysed. The subaltern sections of British capital in consumer-facing services, logistics and manufacturing were also hurt by the contraction in demand generated by the crisis.

The trigger for the financial meltdown was US sub-prime mortgage lending, but its origins lay in the financialised growth model pursued in the US, the UK and many other states around the world. All the morbid symptoms seen since that time – falling investment, stagnant wages, low productivity in the real economy – can be traced back to the logic of finance-led growth – a system based on the use of private debt and speculative investment to conceal the fundamental weaknesses in global capitalism that had emerged by the turn of the century.

Rather than dealing with the underlying issues that led to the 2008 crisis, policymakers attempted to engineer a return to the pre-crisis world. The major capitalist states soon realised that the banks were not simply illiquid (short of cash) but insolvent (completely unable to pay their debts). At this point, they threw their weight behind their financial systems with bailouts that saw states becoming significant shareholders in many of the world's largest financial institutions.

Next, the world's four largest central banks pumped nearly $10 trillion into the financial system by creating new money to buy assets – predominantly their own governments' debt – leading to a new round of asset-price inflation. Quantitative easing prevented the correction in asset prices that should have ensued in the wake of 2008, instead boosting asset values still further through the portfolio rebalancing channel: by substituting government bonds for cash, central banks drove down bond yields and encouraged investors to purchase other assets.[38] Economic stagnation in the Global North, and a slowdown in growth rates elsewhere, constrained productive investment, meaning that much of this capital was directed into the purchase of existing assets such as equities, corporate bonds and property. The result was an increase in equity prices, a corporate debt bubble and a substantial increase in property prices – particularly in London, where property is seen as 'just another asset class'.[39]

In the several years that followed, many countries adopted fiscal stimulus measures to limit the impact of the financial meltdown on the real economy. Initially, the US and the UK both implemented large stimulus programmes aimed at absorbing job losses and preventing the kind of downward spiral in demand that gave us the Great Depression. But it was China that saved the global economy from another depression, with a stimulus package worth nearly 20 per cent of GDP at its peak.[40] Huge state investment protected both the Chinese economy and the economies of its major trading partners.

Then the sovereign debt crisis, which was a delayed response to the financial meltdown of 2008 among countries whose monetary policy was restricted by membership of the euro, hit the PIIGS (Portugal, Italy, Ireland, Greece and Spain). The Troika – the European Commission, the European Central Bank and the International Monetary Fund – imposed harsh austerity measures on countries like Greece in return for bailouts. The UK followed suit and imposed a deep austerity programme, despite there being absolutely no sign of a sovereign debt crisis for the British government. It was these parts of the world that saw some of the deepest stagnation in living standards since the nineteenth century.

The interests of the dominant sections of British capital and the Conservative voter base were largely protected throughout this period by extremely loose monetary policy, which kept the cost of borrowing low. Businesses that otherwise might have gone under were able to stay afloat with cheap credit. Among consumers, those best able to access credit – those with high incomes and existing assets – were the main beneficiaries of low interest rates, which, along with changes to the rules around pensions withdrawals, made it easier for them to acquire more wealth, particularly housing wealth.[41] By combining tight fiscal policy and loose monetary policy, the Conservatives achieved the remarkable feat of protecting the interests of British capital at a time of unique fragility while rebuilding an electoral coalition that has made it the largest party in every election since 2010.

Yet by the time the coronavirus crisis began, the cracks in this model were beginning to show. In the absence of much dynamism in the real economy, loose monetary policy had simply served to prop up asset prices and facilitate what would in any other context look like unsustainable levels of borrowing. Wages in Britain were no higher than they had been in 2007 – a trend that made the ten years since the crash the longest period of wage stagnation since the Napoleonic Wars. Income inequality, meanwhile, was rising – new evidence disproves the received wisdom that it had remained broadly stable since the 1990s.[42]

Wealth inequality was even more extreme, as a small number of extremely rich individuals owned and controlled our corporations, our banks and our land.[43]

It had become impossible for young people to acquire capital in the way that their parents did. The fiscal austerity and productivity crisis that kept wages excessively low made it harder for young people to access mortgages.[44] Many expected never to retire, given the trends in wages and public policy, and even if they did, pension funds were struggling to meet their liabilities in the context of widespread economic stagnation.[45] The financial crisis had generated a unique problem for the neoliberal settlement: why should young people support capitalism when they could never expect to own any capital?

In economies fuelled by consumer spending, the decade after the 2008 financial crisis saw a deepening of the regime of privatised Keynesianism developed before it. Households had become so indebted that permanently low interest rates were required to avoid another crisis, yet permanently low interest rates only led to higher levels of indebtedness. This model is most familiar in Japan and Anglo-America, but over the last twelve years it has spread around the world.[46] A familiar-looking set of challenges emerged in Australia, New Zealand and Canada before the pandemic – the combination of rising household debt, rising real estate prices and a burgeoning current account deficit.[47] Household debt had also started to rise in the Global South, particularly in China.

With profits low, businesses weren't investing or increasing wages. Instead they used the returns they were able to generate, and the cheap debt they were able to raise, to increase payouts to shareholders, buy back

their own shares, merge with or acquire other corporations, or even, in the case of Google and Amazon, buy
up the debt of other corporations – in essence, acting
like banks.[48] Rising corporate debt, combined with the
failure to invest in production, acted as a further brake
on current and future economic growth.

As Richard Koo argues in *The Other Half of
Macroeconomics and the Fate of Globalisation*, the rich
world appeared to be following in the footsteps of Japan
after the bursting of its own debt bubble in the 1990s.[49]
After that debacle, Japan managed to maintain low
rates of growth only through extremely loose monetary
policy, including continuous quantitative easing that
saw the Bank of Japan's balance sheet reach over 100 per
cent of GDP. Such prolonged stagnation is the logical
result of an economic model based on the continuous
growth of private debt that is used for speculation rather
than productive investment. The increase in private debt
in the West ultimately dragged down its investment and
consumption, too. Here the destructive and senseless
logic of austerity in the UK and the Eurozone added to
the malaise.

In the gap between a weak real economy and roaring
asset markets there emerged a mountain of debt. The
global economy was facing a debt overhang (around $244
trillion) many times larger than that which preceded the
financial crisis.[50] Corporate debt, particularly in the US
and the UK, ballooned because of QE and low interest rates. Along with the increase in debt, the continued increase in asset prices driven by quantitative easing
exacerbated pre-existing inequalities and generated a

reaction against globalisation that threatened to bring the whole system crumbling down. With incomes low, savings drained and debt levels high, even an ordinary turn in the business cycle was bound to mean great financial hardship for families throughout the Global North. This was the troubled world upon which the novel coronavirus descended in the first months of 2020.

2

Into State Monopoly Capitalism

In the last week of March 2020, the world's leading central banks pledged to 'do whatever it takes' to bail-out the corporate economy and prevent the bubble in the corporate bond market from bursting. Like quantitative easing after 2008, 'the new Fed backstop for credit for corporate America is here forever', comments one US asset manager.[1] The increasing interpenetration of big business and capitalist states promises to define a new era of state monopoly capitalism, in which the interests of leading politicians, financiers and corporate executives align to such an extent that they come to resemble the 'general cartel' posited by the Austrian economist Rudolf Hilferding in 1910.[2]

Economic crises tend to be moments of market concentration, and the corona crash will see this kind of concentration on steroids. By the end of the crisis, there will be fewer firms left, and those that remain will be much more significant, in terms of both size and political power. The carcasses of small and medium-sized businesses offer juicy pickings for their larger rivals. As Marx wrote, 'capital grows to a huge mass in a single hand in one place, because it has been lost by many in another place'. Marx recognised that the centralisation of capitalism is one of the 'immanent laws of capitalist production itself'.[3] As production becomes ever more capital-intensive, a business's ability to compete rests upon the capacity of its owners to invest in new machinery and technologies. Those larger businesses able to undertake more investment swallow up their smaller rivals, leading to market concentration. This concentration is intensified by the evolution of the credit system – larger firms are able to access more credit and can therefore invest in technologies that allow them to outcompete their rivals. When these smaller firms default, their assets tend to be bought up at rock bottom prices by their larger peers.

On the eve of the First World War, Hilferding predicted that the increasingly close relationships between large firms and financial institutions would ultimately lead to the emergence of a 'unitary power' that would effectively plan capitalist production. Lenin built on his work to analyse how rising market concentration was affecting relations between states: politicians used state power to support the interests of big business until the difference between their interests became difficult to discern. Competition for new markets between state-backed multinational corporations had generated a new age of capitalist imperialism.

After 1945, American militarism ('the arms race') and slick Mad Men marketing underwrote corporate capitalism in its consolidation phase, argued *Monthly Review*'s Paul Baran and Paul Sweezy. But secular stagnation lay

ahead, deferred for a season by a subsequent, unantici-
pated swerve into financialisation in the 1980s, which
destabilised corporate structures – power within a new
'monopoly-finance' hybrid shifting from boardroom
to trading floor. Meanwhile, the US gendarme acted as
ultimate guarantor of neoliberal restructuring on the
periphery.[4]

And today? As Washington escalates its trade-cum-
geopolitical rivalry with the world's second largest economy, and with corporate monopolies headquartered in
the Global North set to dominate ever larger swathes
of the global economy, my argument is this: what has
happened as a result of 2008 and 2020 is that both financial and now also non-financial institutions – in other
words, the entirety of the 'monopoly-finance' hybrid –
have collapsed into the arms of the state, and appear set
to become wholly and permanently reliant upon it.

We have seen how the stabilising of the financial
system after 2008 required not only unprecedented
but prolonged state intervention. Without it, the
international financial system would have collapsed,
bringing down with it large chunks of the real estate
and professional services sectors. Banks were 'too big
to fail' – and the bankers 'too big to jail' – while low
interest rates meant any number of debt-laden corporations were able to survive where otherwise they might
well have collapsed. In effect, by dramatically expanding access to cheap debt, central banks nullified the
Schumpetarian forces that are supposed to regulate
competitive markets, keeping unviable firms alive for

longer.[5] When the inevitable downturn hit in 2020, however, falling revenues had an immediate impact on the delicate balance sheets of so-called 'zombie firms', pushing many into insolvency.[6]

Quantitative easing exacerbated this problem. Higher asset prices encouraged greater levels of lending, while investors' attempts to reach for yield reduced the cost of market finance for many less creditworthy corporations.[7] Observers of US bond markets described what they saw as a bubble waiting to burst. Similar conclusions were drawn in the UK.[8] In fact, ever since the 'Greenspan put' that followed the 1987 stock market crash, investors have counted on the fact that policymakers will hold interest rates down in the wake of a market crash.[9]

Central banks proved unable (some did not even try) to unwind the asset purchasing programmes implemented in response to the 2008 credit crunch. Part of the reason for the ongoing necessity of unorthodox monetary policy was the refusal of many governments – obsessed with the threat posed by the bond vigilantes and their maxims about 'sustainable' rates of borrowing – to use government spending to boost productivity and investment.[10] But another, even more significant, factor was the sheer weakness of the global 'recovery' from the financial crisis itself. Global capitalism had become so sclerotic that policymakers were forced to prop it up with extremely loose monetary policy, which could only influence growth through the roundabout and unsustainable mechanism of artificially boosting lending and asset prices.

Banks, businesses and investors knew that when the next crisis hit, central bankers would have no choice but to loosen monetary policy still further. Zombie firms lingered on thanks to the largesse of central bankers, while international monopolies profited from restricting production, exploiting workers under conditions of low pay and avoiding tax. Marx's warnings about big capital's ability to generate even greater levels of 'misery, oppression, slavery, degradation and exploitation' seemed to be coming true.[11]

How does this characterisation fit with the glamorous image from which many tech firms have benefited in the last few years? Many tech companies are hugely popular with users because they provide useful services for free or at very low prices. It would be very difficult for these companies to generate supernormal profits from selling a service that can be produced at zero marginal cost: if Google started to charge customers for searching the web, users would simply migrate to another search engine, which could easily expand to accommodate the new demand. As a result, the prices of many digital services are low, or zero.

But while the dynamics of production at zero marginal cost lead to lower prices, they also generate tendencies towards monopoly and rentierisation.[12] This is because the business models of the big tech giants do not rest on the provision of free digital services – a strategy from which no profit could be generated. Instead, they collect an extremely valuable commodity produced by their users – data – and sell it on to advertisers, researchers and states.[13] The extraction and commodification of this data by the big tech giants is a new method for the generation of economic rents.[14] Business models based on the monopolisation of a particular online 'space' use network effects to establish near total market dominance. Monopoly power is then exploited to acquire users' data for free, often without sufficient privacy safeguards. Prices do not seem to exceed the costs of production, so neoclassical economists cannot detect the existence of a monopoly – yet workers, suppliers, taxpayers and even consumers still suffer as a result.

The big tech companies have also engaged in other practices designed to consolidate their monopoly power. Some use anti-competitive practices designed to penalise their rivals, most use various accounting mechanisms to avoid taxation in order to boost their profits, and almost all have cosy relationships with local and national governments, which often allow them to access preferential treatment denied to their competitors.[15] States stood by as these companies became ever more powerful, often providing them with subsidies, turning a blind eye to regulatory arbitrage and competing with one another to attract their investment.

As the coronavirus pandemic has deepened, the big tech companies have emerged as some of the greatest beneficiaries. Microsoft, Apple, Alphabet, Amazon and Facebook now make up a fifth of the entire value of the S&P 500 Index, and Jeff Bezos is on track to become the world's first trillionaire.[16] Part of the reason these companies' stocks are doing so well is that their business models, to varying extents, render them immune from the impact of the virus-induced lockdown. Given that they provide many of their services and sell many of their products online, most have not seen a fall in sales. In fact, some of these firms have seen a spike in demand as housebound consumers flock online to work, consume and entertain themselves. Amazon has taken on 175,000 extra staff to cope with the rising number of orders.

But many of these shares were outperforming the rest of the stock market even before the crisis. Some analysts argued that we were seeing another bubble in big tech. Others claimed that the strength of the tech companies' business models meant that their high current valuations were justified. There is a third explanation. It is not the strength of these companies' business models per se that explains their high stock prices and apparent invulnerability to crisis, but their market power. Investors were behaving rationally when they piled money into companies like Amazon, but only because they could see that the company was rapidly becoming one of the most powerful monopolies in human history.

Monopolies can only become monopolies if they are able to access the investment needed to gain total market dominance – and as the twenty-first century has progressed, this has proven easier than ever, especially in big tech. The tech companies emerged in a world of falling profits and associated rising volatility in financial markets – both of which facilitated their access to investment. Many of these companies were initially either unprofitable or loss-making, as they had not yet developed to a sufficient size to exploit the network effects that would provide the foundation for their monopoly power. As a result, they required significant amounts of upfront investment to maintain their operations and to scale up to reach a position of market dominance that would allow them to turn a profit.

The most propitious time for these firms to access such investment was in the wake of a crisis that had depressed returns and when investors were desperately seeking out the next big thing – for the tech companies, this meant either the tech crisis of the early 2000s, after which Google launched its IPO, or the financial crisis of 2008, after which many companies went public, including Facebook and Twitter.[17] The cheap capital – in part a result of unorthodox monetary policy – swashing around the global economy in the wake of a financial crisis that had depressed returns everywhere provided the perfect conditions for these plucky tech companies to become the behemoths we know today. Just a few years ago, Amazon was struggling to turn a profit – now it is completely unassailable.

Today, the capital that would be required to compete with a company like Alphabet or Facebook is unimaginably large. Their sheer scale is what allows these companies to maintain their monopoly positions, even as many consumers express dissatisfaction with the services they are providing. These firms simply have too much money for anyone to be able to challenge them – their market capitalisations are larger than the GDP of the average state. After years of generating supernormal profits in an otherwise depressed economic environment, many of these firms – alongside monopolies in more traditional industries – are sitting on huge piles of cash, much of which they are unable – or unwilling – to invest in innovation or production. The resultant 'corporate savings glut' poses a significant theoretical challenge to economists and is a source of concern for policymakers.[18]

In fact, the corporate savings glut is accelerating the financialisation of the average monopoly by inverting the usual relationship between financial institutions and corporations. Rather than simply enabling companies to access capital from sceptical investors, many financial institutions are now helping large firms invest their 'savings' in financial markets. Rana Foroohar pointed out in the *Financial Times* in 2018 that, far from hoarding cash, the big tech giants, and many other large monopolies, were using their earnings to buy up corporate and government bonds.[19] Some companies were taking advantage of their relationships with banks to take on new debt and invest it in riskier, higher-yielding corporate bonds elsewhere in the world.

The world described by economists – in which household savings are used to finance corporate borrowing – is turned upside down in the era of monopoly capitalism, with households taking on ever greater debts and corporations sitting on ever greater profits. And the links between business and finance go deeper – the investment banks that manage these corporations' financial affairs, and the investors who own their shares, have made a killing. But today, the tech companies, less regulated and more popular than the investment banks, are increasingly the leading partners in a relationship where they were once merely clients.

It is not simply the nature of the market that benefits large businesses over smaller ones, but also the nature of the state. The bigger the business, the deeper its political connections, and the more likely it is both to survive a crisis and to gain access to state support if it struggles. While many small businesses have struggled to access government loans during the pandemic, larger corporations – with much closer relationships to government – have benefited from the extremely cheap liquidity being provided by the major central banks. Renewed quantitative easing will keep down the costs of market financing by repressing the yields on corporate bonds, providing a boost to businesses and their investors. Regardless of their productivity, the sustainability of their business models or their environmental impact, the world's largest firms will exit the current crisis with even more market power than they currently have. But the level of support being provided suggests that central banks are creating a problem of moral hazard – shielding investors, banks and businesses from the risks they took during the upswing of the economic cycle as soon as the downturn begins.[20]

Many though certainly not all corporations may also be rescued by outright nationalisation, to tide them over this sticky patch. The airline industry is a case in point. It is one of the sectors that has been worst hit by the pandemic, and is also of strategic importance to states that wish to remain embedded within the global economy. As a result, airlines – many of which were set up by states in the post-war period before being privatised in the 1980s and 1990s – have been some of the first companies to be nationalised as a result of the pandemic. In Germany, after entering into talks with struggling national carrier Lufthansa, the Merkel government stated its willingness to nationalise both Lufthansa and Condor. The French government, a shareholder in Air France-KLM, was in talks with Air France about a possible full nationalisation of the company. Italy had already taken full control over Alitalia. And with airlines like British Airways, Singapore Airlines and Cathay Pacific all having been forced to ground more than 90 per cent of their fleets, more nationalisations are likely to follow, even allowing for a destabilising Lehman Brothers-type exception to the rule, possibly involving the likes of Virgin Atlantic.

The present combination of state-provided liquidity and full-on bailouts mirrors the extraordinary interventions undertaken by states in the Global North to save their finance sectors in 2008 – only this time, the money is being directed towards the entire corporate sector. Moral hazard is a genuine issue – irresponsible lenders and uncreditworthy businesses are being protected by the state – but no one is seriously suggesting that the global economy be allowed to implode. States and central banks are now being forced to engage in the active planning of their entire economies under the imperial coordination of the Federal Reserve. Except that the planning that is taking place is neither democratic nor rational.

In the US, the Coronavirus Aid, Relief and Economic Security (CARES) Act which bailed out non-financial corporations is riddled with 'ambiguity of language, inconsistencies, loopholes and qualifications', writes

Robert Brenner. 'The equivalent of two and a half times US annual corporate profits, or about 20 per cent of US annual GDP, was authorized to be dispensed without undue surveillance and with no strings attached.'[21]

Elites are huddling in smoke-filled rooms to decide which companies will fail and which will survive, and how much of our collective resources will be used to save them. These decisions are not being based on rational calculation – no consideration is being made, for example, of the environmental sustainability, tax practices or employment practices of the companies in question – but on the demands of various vested interests.

As capitalism has become more centralised, the defining justification for its existence – that competition between firms promotes the most efficient use of society's scarce resources – has ceased to apply. Adam Smith's 'invisible hand' has been replaced by the iron fist of the modern monopoly, supported by the capitalist state, which has succeeded in extracting huge amounts of value from workers all over the world. When markets are dominated by a few large firms, and when state action is the only thing that stands between a firm and bankruptcy, it is hard to argue that resource allocation continues to be governed by free market competition. Instead, decisions about the production and allocation of resources are effectively made by a small number of people at the top of the world's largest corporations. Ongoing centralisation during the pandemic will strengthen links between business and the state on the one hand – states will become more dependent upon these businesses for tax revenues and political funding, while the businesses will become more interested in regulation and tax policy – and businesses and the banks that manage their cash on the other. In other words, we will increasingly see private planning of the economy. Free market, competitive capitalism – if it ever actually existed – is dead.

Many economic libertarians would recognise this critique. They frequently complain about moral hazard and loose monetary policy, blaming the overactivity of the state for the emergence of a form of 'crony capitalism' characterised by market centralisation, complex regulation and low productivity, and arguing for a return to a purer, more competitive, freer version of capitalism. These arguments are generally pitted against those of social democrats, who respond that state intervention is necessary to mitigate the ups and downs of the business cycle – to protect workers from the caprices of capitalist accumulation. Banks, businesses and investors must be bailed out because otherwise the entire economic system will collapse, bringing civilisation down with it.[22] Both arguments have some merit. Excessive state intervention has distorted the operation of free market capitalism, helping to transform it into a financialised, monopolistic variant. However, without the interventions that have given rise to such a situation, the global economy would likely have collapsed, with far-reaching political implications.

The apparent contradiction between these two arguments is, however, only superficial. Proponents of both perspectives rely upon the liberal notion that the political and the economic are somehow separate – that free markets exist as a self-regulating sphere, subject to greater or lesser levels of intervention from a central state.[23] The rigid ideological separation between politics and economics – states and markets – helps to legitimise liberal capitalism. State activity is framed as 'intervention' in a self-contained, self-regulating market system. More often than not, such interventions – it is argued – throw the system off course. A state that provides a strong social safety net threatens to erode the desperate reserve army of labour that capital relies upon to generate profits and discipline workers, so those on the right argue that unions and minimum wage laws disrupt the operation of the free market.

But how can this line of reasoning be sustained when business, finance and workers are so dependent upon the state that, if it ceased coordinating economic activity, the entire economy would collapse? If the state could afford to spend billions of pounds bailing out the country's wealthy bankers, then why shouldn't it provide free higher education, housing and healthcare when the crisis ends? The separation between politics and economics cannot be sustained in such a situation. States will never again be able to respond to demands for higher wages, better public services and relief for the vulnerable by claiming that these things are unaffordable, unworkable or unsustainable. At the end of this crisis, management of the economy will be irreversibly politicised.

In this context, the suggestion that governments must refrain from 'interfering' in the forces of free market competition to create jobs, reduce inequality and increase environmental sustainability is laughable. We do not live in a competitive economy – we live in a planned economy. But the planning is not democratic – it is being undertaken by central bankers, senior politicians and their advisors in big business and finance. It is no coincidence that in recent years the Federal Reserve and the European Central Bank have both hired Blackrock – the largest asset manager in the world, for which former UK Chancellor of the Exchequer George Osborne works – to manage their asset purchasing schemes.[24] At times of crisis, it becomes very obvious that global capitalism is run by a tiny cabal, who use their power not to promote market efficiency or competition, but to promote their own narrow self-interest.

The revival of the British Left was based on a critique of a kind of state, and indeed a kind of capitalism, that is unlikely to exist when this crisis is over. Socialists have grown used to campaigning against cuts to government spending, but these lines will ring hollow in the war economy created by the pandemic, in which the government is spending a great deal to support the interests of big business and finance. The challenge we face is not agitating for more state intervention. We cannot fall into the trap, outlined by Lenin, of believing that a quantitative increase in state activity somehow affects a qualitative shift from capitalism to socialism. Instead, we must concern ourselves with how state power is being used – and who is wielding it. By the end of this crisis, a tiny oligarchy of politicians, central bankers, financiers and corporate executives will have further monopolised wealth and power in the global economy. The challenge for the Left will be to hold them to account.

3

The New Imperialism

At the end of the 1980s, as the Iron Curtain fell and free market capitalism spread to most parts of the world, Francis Fukuyama declared the end of history. The evangelists of capital promised an era of opportunity and prosperity, including for poorer nations.[1] The 2008 financial crisis shattered this illusion and brought history back with a bang. Resistance to globalisation, once confined to protest movements in the Global South and anarchists in the Global North, began to mount in the very states most integrated into the global economy.

But while the Left benefited from the backlash against capitalism that emerged after the 2008 crash, the Right was more likely to benefit from the backlash against globalisation. The ease with which these two processes have been separated exposes the weakness of the Left's critique of capitalism since the decline of the anti-globo movement – because, in fact, globalisation and capitalism are inseparable.

While the economies of the Global North have transitioned away from commodities production, the horrifying working practices that Marx described in

Capital have not disappeared: they have simply been moved out of the sight of the modern consumer. After several decades of neoliberal outsourcing, the workshops of the world now exist in China, where Foxconn installed nets at its factories to catch those who attempted suicide; in Bangladesh, where a collapsing textile factory killed over a thousand workers; and in the Democratic Republic of Congo, where child labour is used to mine the coltan used in our mobile phones and computers.

Nowadays entire economies specialise in the management of this exploitative globalised production process. Marx commented upon the role of the manager – the privileged workers who 'command during the labour process in the name of capital'.[2] Such workers could be relied upon to support the interests of capital, despite the exploitation that marks their relationship with their bosses, because their higher wages and social status are premised upon the hyper-exploitation of those beneath them.[3] In many states across Europe and North America – especially Britain and the United States – a large professional-managerial class, mostly employed in finance and professional services, has emerged since the 1980s. The average member of the professional-managerial class may work in the head office of a large multinational corporation managing a production process that takes place elsewhere, as a trader in an investment bank speculating on surplus value generated elsewhere, or as an advertising specialist advising corporations on how best to realise surplus value generated elsewhere. But for every nation of managers, there are dozens of nations of hyper-exploited workers kept in check by repressive states and monitoring technologies.[4]

What we today call globalisation has commonalities with the process of imperialism that Lenin examined a hundred years ago.[5] Rather than investing domestically – where returns were lower, owing to both lower rates of growth and the existence of taxes, regulation and strong labour movements – financiers would help to channel the capital accumulated by monopolists into the periphery of the world economy, where the transition to capitalism was not yet complete. Competition would not die under state monopoly capitalism – mega-firms never merge entirely into one. Instead, they continue to engage in limited forms of competition with one another at the global rather than simply the domestic level, supported by governments who engage in inter-state competition in order to secure new markets into which domestic capital can expand. This, Lenin contended, was the basis of imperialism, 'the highest stage of capitalism'.[6]

Today's global monopolies sit on huge piles of cash generated from their anti-competitive practices, with the support of imperial states. They then distribute vast sums to wealthy shareholders, using only some of what remains for productive investment, and the rest to buy back their own shares or merge with or acquire other corporations. Just as Lenin would have expected, capital flows from North to South have allowed wealthy investors to buy up assets in the periphery and profit from growth in these states. The imperialist circle is completed when the profits created by this process are sent back to financial institutions in the Global North. Sub-Saharan Africa, for example, loses three times more in capital flight than it gains in 'development' aid each year.[7]

This geographical pattern is not coincidental. Those states first to industrialise were the first to build multinational corporations and organised work-forces, which won a series of victories that pushed up the price of their labour-power. States supported domestic corporations in accessing cheap labour and new markets abroad, first through military and then through political-economic imperialism: asymmetric trade and investment treaties, the reshoring of inter-national profits and pressure to adopt 'free market' economic policies from wealthy states and the interna-tional organisations they support.[8]

The international division of labour under contem-porary globalisation continues to be structured by imperialistic relationships between states. The value chains used by many large monopolies engaged in commodities production span the globe – low value-added activities take place in the periphery, where profits are often generated, while high value-added activities take place in the core, where profits are repat-riated.[9] For 'tech' firms like Apple, which derive most of their profits from ordinary commodity production, these relationships are very obvious: hyper-exploited Foxconn workers in China manufacture iPhones while largely unproductive workers in the 'head office' located in the US benefit from inflated wages.[10]

Although it is far from consensual, modern-day imperialism is not primarily enforced using violence. 'The neo-colonialism of today represents imperialism in its final and perhaps its most dangerous stage', argued Kwame Nkrumah, Ghana's independence leader, in 1965. 'The essence of neocolonialism is that the state which is subject to it is, in theory, independent and has all the outward trappings of international sovereignty. In reality its economic system and thus its political policy is directed from outside.'[11]

Neocolonial power is exercised through two interlinked processes: the domination of Western monopolies over the markets of the Global South (process 1), and the transfer of any profits that do accrue to domestic capital in the Global South to the Global North through extractive networks linked to major financial centres like the City of London (process 2). While process 1 dominated during the Bretton Woods era, process 2 has become much more important in the era of financial globalisation.

The pivot came with the Third World debt crisis of the 1970s and 1980s, a result of oil-price shocks and rising interest rates in the West, which forced debt-distressed countries such as Ghana to implement pro-market reforms in exchange for debt relief.[12] The debt crisis was used as an opportunity to 'open up' poorer countries to international investment – a euphemism for preventing democratically elected governments from embarking upon state-led development programmes in favour of the external enforcement of 'market friendly' policies that would benefit international capital.

Structural adjustment programmes often negatively impacted human and economic development – especially in sub-Saharan Africa.[13] The much-touted effects on economic growth turned out to be negligible, while the poorest were hit hardest by cuts to infrastructure, education and public services.[14] Over the long term, the debt crisis and structural adjustment programmes curtailed incomes and economic growth, as capital fled the Global South. As a result, the size of these nations' debts only increased relative to their GDP.

Capital account liberalisation – enforced through structural adjustment – was supposed to assist 'developing' economies in pursuing a strategy of 'export-led growth'. Mainstream economists claimed that low-income countries should focus on their 'comparative advantage' by exporting commodities to the rest of the world – which meant ending subsidies to domestic industry, 'freeing' the private sector from regulation and state intervention, and removing constraints on capital mobility. In fact, these measures simply made it easier for multinational corporations to enter the economies of the Global South and displace domestic capitalists before reshoring their profits to the Global North. It also made it easier for elites to siphon their cash out of the country and store it abroad, often in tax havens. Meanwhile, domestic producers faced huge barriers to exporting their goods on a global market weighted towards core countries, which used their huge resources to protect their domestic producers.

But it is not simply the Global South that has been harmed by financial globalisation. Capital flows from the periphery into the imperial core have also warped the economies of core countries[15] and increased the risk of financial crisis.[16] According to textbook economic theory, large imbalances between creditor countries with large current account surpluses and debtors with large current account deficits should be self-correcting. When a country runs a deficit, currency is flowing out of the country. If this currency does not return, the resulting increase in supply will exert downward pressure on the currency. A less valuable currency makes your exports cheaper to international consumers and should therefore increase demand for those exports. Played out over the scale of the global economy, this should lead to equilibrium. In the lead-up to the 2008 financial crisis, the fact that this equilibrium was not forthcoming puzzled some economists. Deficit countries should have been experiencing large currency depreciations, given the size of their current account deficits. These depreciations should, in turn, then have increased the competitiveness of their goods. Ben Bernanke of the Federal Reserve accused a number of emerging economies of hoarding savings to protect themselves from future crises, preventing the global economy from reaching equilibrium.

In fact, these global imbalances emerged directly from the imperialistic relationships that define global capitalism. Beginning in the late 1990s, the volume of capital flowing out of the Global South exceeded the volume of capital flowing into it in the form of foreign direct investment – in other words, process 2 has begun to dominate process 1 – largely due to the dynamics of capital flight and tax avoidance.[17] The capital that flowed back into the financial centres of the Global North was then used to support the domestic processes of financialisation.[18] Deficit countries were able to maintain strong currencies because, even though there was relatively little demand for their goods, there was strong demand for their assets – particularly financial assets. The main reason for the high demand for these assets – especially in the US and the UK – was the financial deregulation undertaken by neoliberal governments in these states in the 1980s, which facilitated a dramatic expansion in the provision of private credit to individuals, businesses and financial institutions.[19] Ultimately, much of this lending was driven by the emergence of a bubble in US and UK property markets, combined with the weakening of bank regulation meant to limit the emergence of such fragilities. Capital from the rest of the world flowed into the finance sectors of the Global North seeking out higher returns, allowing this bubble to expand even further.

Zambia, which has a long history of difficult relations with the international financial institutions, offers a good example of how modern imperialism has stunted the development of many states in the Global South. An economy highly reliant on the export of copper, Zambia was hit hard by the commodities price crash in the 1970s. Unable to borrow on international financial markets, Zambia was forced to go to the IMF for financial assistance, and was placed on a structural adjustment programme. It was accorded 'middle income

country' status in 2011 but few of the population benefited from the GDP growth of this period. Debt levels
and inequality have worsened. The country remains
dependent upon copper exports and unable to generate the capital necessary to industrialise.[20] Zambia has
been forced to deal with even less scrupulous lenders.
One of the vulture funds which buy up the debt of
poor countries that look likely to default, in the hope
of suing them for huge sums of money, bought up $3
million worth of Zambian debt and then, in 2007,
successfully sued the country for $15 million.[21]

When copper prices tanked as the pandemic hit
global demand for commodities, the Zambian currency
(the kwacha) fell with them, increasing the cost of its
debt servicing.[22] Without much global demand for
copper, and with remittances and FDI flows having
halted almost entirely, the country cannot access
enough foreign currency to repay creditors. Over the
longer term, it is highly likely that Zambia's debts
are too high ever to be repaid. Much of its outstanding debt is owed to Chinese state-owned banks – as a
relatively new large lender, it is unclear how China will
respond to calls from Africa for debt restructuring.

Meanwhile, on the other side of the South Atlantic,
Argentina under left-wing Peronist president Alberto
Fernández, elected in 2019, is undergoing its ninth
sovereign default. Like other economies in the Global
South, international institutions have allied with the
bond vigilantes to bludgeon Argentina into imposing policies that benefit international investors and
harm working people. The threat that the Fernandez

government might impose restrictions on capital mobility was causing significant concern among investors even before the pandemic. They sought to discipline the struggling state into submission by selling Argentinian assets. Bond yields spiked and the currency depreciated, making borrowing much more expensive.

It is unlikely that either Argentina or Zambia will be able to escape the current crisis on its own. States in debt distress of this scale need cheap, long-term, unconditional lending to fund investment that can boost productivity and competitiveness. But the structure of the imperialist international system – built in the interests of the 'bond vigilantes' – militates against this.[23]

The Global South is now fighting a battle against nature on two fronts: not only tackling the spread of the coronavirus but also dealing with the effects of climate breakdown. The challenge these states face was made abundantly clear when Cyclone Amphan struck India and Bangladesh in May 2020. India, a middle-income country with high levels of poverty, had more than 100,000 confirmed cases of Covid-19 and 3,000 deaths at the time of the disaster, while Bangladesh, one of the poorest countries in the world, had nearly 27,000 confirmed cases and around 400 deaths. Both states have weak public health infrastructures. They have struggled to roll out measures such as mass testing owing to state under-capacity and to achieve social distancing given the cramped living conditions faced by many families.[24] The mass evacuations associated with Cyclone Amphan will only increase the challenge. Meanwhile, those working in the informal economy, migrant workers and the industrial working class have suffered immensely during the lockdown, which has constrained already-low incomes and left many people destitute.

In the Global North, the answer to climate change and the coronavirus is simple: spend. When these states are hit by extreme weather events – flooding in the United Kingdom, the recent spate of fires in Australia or the increasing frequency of hurricanes and storms in the United States – they pay out billions to contain the economic impact. In response to the pandemic, they are spending unprecedented amounts of money and further loosening monetary policy to support their domestic capitalist class – and in the case of the United States, the international capitalist class.

Many on the Left have argued that the scale of the fiscal response in the Global North proves what they have been arguing for years: that governments face no strict limits on their spending.[25] They can issue bonds and create money to spend away, only keeping an eye on inflation to ensure that the economy does not overheat. This narrative comes up against one major problem: it applies only to the Global North. States in the Global South will be less able to insulate themselves from the economic impact of the virus. They could see their healthcare and limited social security systems overwhelmed by the pandemic – either they will respond, meaning more borrowing from foreign creditors, or they will not, meaning that output will take a substantial hit. But at the very moment that workers all over the world are relying on states to increase their spending on public services and social security, investors are fleeing 'emerging markets', concerned about the economic impact of the coronavirus.

The scale of the outflows is in part due to the significant inflows many emerging-market economies experienced after the 2008 financial crisis had battered the economies of the Global North.[26] The post-2008 excitement about the BRICS (Brazil, Russia, India, China and South Africa) – and latterly, the MINTs (Mexico, Indonesia, Nigeria and Turkey) – saw large sums of money flow into the Global South. Countries in the periphery of the world system had been less severely affected by the financial crisis than those in the North and were also benefiting from China's huge post-crisis stimulus package. Low interest rates and unconventional monetary policy in the Global North also sent investors reaching for yield – seeking out investment opportunities that would provide them with higher returns.[27] Sometimes this capital sought out genuinely useful infrastructure projects; sometimes it was lent to foreign governments; and sometimes it was channelled into real estate or used for pure speculation.

Before the coronavirus crisis, the IMF reported that 40 per cent of low-income countries were either in or approaching debt distress.[28] The concern then was that interest rate rises in the Global North would lead to a round of capital flight like that which sparked the 1980s Global South debt crisis. The pandemic has not led to an increase in interest rates in the Global

North, but it has catalysed a flight to safety among investors, who are flooding into dollar-denominated assets. In May 2020, the IMF informed the world that the Global South was facing the biggest capital outflow ever recorded.[29] Capital flight has increased bond yields for states in the Global South and compromised their debt sustainability.[30] Many of these same states will struggle to meet their liabilities to international investors. The contraction in international trade flows and remittances will reduce their incomes, and their spending will have to increase in order to contain the impact of the virus. If they cannot access the foreign currency many of them need to pay their debts, these states may tip closer into insolvency.

The IMF's managing director, Kristalina Georgieva, has said that the fund has $1trn worth of resources to help its members tackle the pandemic, on top of the $160 billion in loans and grants already promised by the World Bank. But not all countries are eligible for these loans: preferential treatment is given to obedient adopters of the free trade and market based Washington Consensus.

Unlike other poor countries, many of which are currently in deep debt distress, international investors have not yet turned on India and Bangladesh. As one of the first countries to implement the required neoliberal 'reforms', Bangladesh became something of a poster child for structural adjustment, even though poverty remains high.[31] Today the country is highly dependent upon textiles manufacturing, where working conditions are notoriously poor, leading to disasters like the 2013

Dhaka factory collapse. In India, Modi's election was greeted with delight by the international community, given his business-friendly rhetoric and his commitment to pushing through long-awaited free market 'reforms'. But many investors have been disappointed by the slow progress of Modi's reform agenda, as the Hindu nationalist prime minister has instead focused on persecuting the country's Muslim minority.[32]

Both countries have been able to mount some economic response to the coronavirus. Modi's government announced a bailout package worth over $260 billion – around 10 per cent of India's yearly output.[33] Having locked down the country with less than four hours' notice, stranding the poor without food or work, in June the government began unwinding restrictions even before the peak of infections had been reached. Bangladesh announced several fiscal measures worth nearly $8 billion[34] – or 2.5 per cent of the country's GDP – but began to reopen many of its textile factories early to boost exports, potentially worsening the spread of the virus and putting workers' lives in jeopardy.

Over the long term, as the coronavirus crisis continues and the impact of climate breakdown begins to hit both nations, the favour of international investors will do little to help these states. The response to both crises will require a significant increase in government borrowing, potentially leading to a loss of confidence among notoriously fickle bond investors. But without significant increases in state spending, tens of thousands more people could be killed over the coming years by both coronavirus and the increasing frequency and severity of natural disasters associated with climate breakdown.

The Global South is continuously promised that, if it only sticks to the prescriptions delivered by the institutions of the Washington Consensus – the IMF and the World Bank – it will 'catch up' with the Global North. In fact, ongoing neocolonial and imperialistic relationships between the Global North and South, not to mention the huge amount of money that escapes the world's poorest states through money laundering and tax avoidance, have prevented most states in the global South from doing so – and the growth of the tech monopolies has only made these problems worse.[35] Rigid followers of the Washington Consensus have sacrificed the health and well-being of their workers to increase the profits of international capital. China and other East Asian developmental states are some of the only countries that have managed to escape the trap of neocolonialism and dependency by ignoring the advice of the international financial institutions and focusing on state-led development.

For the rich world, the lesson of the coronavirus crisis is that states can spend to meet the needs of their populations without limit. For the vast majority of the world's population, this crisis will simply reinforce what they already knew: that the poorer, less powerful members of the international 'community' most certainly can't. Socialists in the Global North must learn the right lesson: that the limits of fiscal policy are determined by political power. International solidarity requires us to return to the issue of debt forgiveness and push for relief for Global South states when this crisis is over.

The issue of debt cancellation has been central to what was once known as the 'Third World movement' since its inception. Activists have been campaigning for the cancellation of 'odious debts' for years. They achieved some success with the millennium debt campaign, but for many countries it was not nearly enough.[36] Even a significant programme of IMF lending to counter the impact of the immediate financial crisis ripping through the Global South will not be sufficient to deal with the long-term issue of debt sustainability. Piling new debt on top of old debt is not going to allow poor states to escape the cycle of debt and dependency that many have endured since independence. What is needed is a debt write-off.[37]

In April 2020, G20 finance ministers agreed to halt debt servicing payments for low-income countries until the end of the year. But a payment pause will simply delay the pain until later in the year, when the global economy is likely to remain in a deep depression.[38] Moreover, the initiative didn't include all bilateral lenders. Certain states and financial institutions that own significant chunks of Global South debt have been asked to work constructively with debtors during the pandemic, but they have no obligation to do so.

From the structural adjustment programmes of the 1980s to modern-day Greece, the long arm of the imperial creditor has been used many times to subject peripheral states to the discipline of capital. The coronavirus pandemic will only deepen these relationships of imperial extraction.

4

Reconstruction

It is often said that, in the midst of a crisis, everyone is a socialist. With massive state intervention now the only thing standing between economies battered by the coronavirus pandemic and global economic meltdown, few politicians or economists are calling on governments to step back, let businesses fail, banks go bust and homeowners default on their mortgages – even if some countries have attempted to extricate themselves from lockdown and return to 'business as usual' before getting the virus under control.[1]

In normal times, neoliberals have a knee-jerk reaction against any interference in the operation of supposedly free, competitive markets. Too much public investment distorts the natural operation of the price mechanism, which facilitates the efficient allocation of society's resources by maintaining an equilibrium between supply and demand, they argue. To counter this problem, states would have to know exactly how many resources were available and have a concrete plan for how they would be used. The economy is too complex a system to be subject to successful central planning. Any well-intentioned bureaucratic interventions would have unintended consequences that would be more likely to decrease efficiency than bolster it.

Public ownership of or public support for private firms, meanwhile, interferes with the Schumpetarian forces of creative destruction that provide the basis of capitalism's dynamism, according to right-wing economists. Subsidies or cheap loans for businesses producing environmentally sustainable products or researching new technologies would remove any incentive these firms might have to use their resources efficiently. Corporate governance would suffer as these firms became subject to corruption and clientelism owing to their increasingly close relationships with state actors. Bureaucrats and their friends in state-backed private corporations would use their power to serve their own interests. The Green New Deal would, according to free market ideologists, only lead to corruption and inefficiency of the kind that would *worsen* environmental breakdown.

But the strength of these arguments is called into question by the evidence about how actually existing capitalism functions. The system is already characterised by widespread collusion between international monopolies and their clients in state and international institutions, with all the corruption and inefficiency this entails. Financial, corporate and political elites work together to plan economic activity – but they do so in their own interests, rather than in the public interest.

Governments are providing emergency subsidies, cheap loans and occasionally full-blown bailouts to firms that have swelled to vast proportions, absorbing smaller businesses in their wake and flouting environmental and labour regulation, as well as failing to pay tax. Meanwhile, central banks are playing a significant role in planning the allocation of capital in the economy, but they have been doing so in order to inflate asset prices and to provide cheap credit to the entire private sector, regardless of how this credit is used. Fossil fuel companies are lobbying hard for state aid, while polluting businesses have found it easy to access cheap loans. Any number of companies that provide useless, or actively harmful, goods and services – often in highly inefficient ways – have survived through state largesse where otherwise they would have failed. This is the reality of state monopoly capitalism.

We must learn to understand capitalism as a holistic system – one in which states, capitalists and other powerful ruling class actors cooperate in order to ensure their own survival, and the survival of the system that created them. Capitalist states, banks and enterprises work together during moments of crisis to protect one another from the consequences of their actions, and to limit the impact of the downturn so as to forestall demands for fundamental political and economic transformation. The links between big business, finance and government do not represent a perversion of liberal democracy; they are an increasingly unavoidable feature of capitalist political economy. Wealth translates into influence, and influence back into wealth. There are no nonpolitical solutions to economic problems: every economic question is a question of power.

The question then arises – if we are already living in a planned economy, shouldn't those making the decisions be subject to scrutiny? Shouldn't the plans that determine how we live our lives be decided democratically? The monopolisation of global capitalism that results from this crisis will force these questions of power and ownership to the centre of public debate. But the global monopolies, and the imperialist states that support them, will not give up their power without a fight.

The only way to counter the oligarchic tendencies now emerging within many Western democracies is to deepen the accountability of public officials to working people, and to democratize the economy itself. Government departments, central banks and quasi nongovernmental organizations must all be subject to much deeper public scrutiny. We also need to introduce public ownership and democratic control of our largest corporations and financial institutions. If the government does embark upon a programme of mass bailouts, the corporations it saves should be run by the people, not just a tiny elite. The aim of such a democratic agenda would be to decarbonise our economies while raising living standards and reducing inequality.

Free marketeers will trot out the same arguments against such plans, but they will be confronted by the reality that we already live in an uncompetitive, monopolistic and state-planned economy. They may argue for a return to a different kind of capitalism, but unless they are able to chart a course to actually get there – impossible without huge social and political costs – their arguments will be untenable. Socialists must begin to make the case for a democratic Green New Deal now by pointing to the level of state planning currently underway in response to the coronavirus crisis – planning that has to a lesser extent been in place for years and will likely continue for many years to come. The line between 'state' and 'market' – constructed by liberal political economy – is now thinner than ever. Our choice is not 'to plan or not to plan?' but 'in whose interests should we plan?'

If socialism meant corporate welfare, we would be entering a massive socialist revival. But socialism is not, of course, corporate welfare. Suggestions that greater levels of state intervention will automatically deliver socialism must be dismissed. Capitalist states cannot simply transform themselves into socialist ones through temporary labour market interventions and strategic nationalisations. No matter how much a government spends on healthcare and education – or, in this context, furlough schemes and business loans – it will never become a socialist state. 'The bourgeois reformist view that monopoly capitalism or state-monopoly capitalism is no longer capitalism, but can already be termed "state socialism" or something of that sort, is a very widespread error', observed Lenin in *The State and Revolution* (1917). 'But however much of a plan they may create', he added, 'we still remain under capitalism – capitalism, it is true, in its new stage, but still, unquestionably, capitalism.'

Without emergency action by governments, the coronavirus crisis would have immediately spiralled beyond all control. Fire sales of assets undertaken either by desperate debtors or during insolvency proceedings would have catalysed a process of debt deflation, where falling asset prices increase the real value of outstanding debts.[2] Seeing the value of their assets fall relative to their liabilities, even formerly creditworthy households, businesses and financial institutions would have found themselves facing insolvency. This debt-deflationary cycle was avoided at the cost of providing near-unlimited support and guarantees to corporations and financial institutions – in other words, corporate welfare designed to save capitalism from itself.

The support that has been offered to workers must be viewed through the same lens. In the UK, consumer spending makes up around 65 per cent of GDP.[3] Without workers to buy cars, houses, clothes, TVs, meals out and the plethora of other consumer goods now available to nearly everyone thanks to the dramatic expansion in debt-fuelled spending that has taken place since the 1980s, the economy would collapse. Businesses would fail to realize the profits generated in production, default on their loans and bring the banks down with them. The British state is spending more because British capitalists – and indeed capitalists around the world – need it to spend more. As Gary Stevenson argues, 'the government has created new money to replace the lost spending of the rich, so that working people can continue to pay their bills to the rich'.[4] This spending will continue for as long as it continues to benefit the wealthy – and not for a minute longer.

The fundamental character of political power in any country is always determined by the balance of power between labour and capital, and the way in which this balance is institutionalised. The recent unprecedented interventions of the British state have supported the interests of the coalition that underpins finance-led growth: big capitalists and homeowners. The financial system is, as always, supported with every state resource available, and corporations have been given access to a near-endless pool of liquidity. Meanwhile mortgage holders were quickly provided with a three-month break on their mortgage payments.

Under pressure from the trade union movement, Chancellor Rishi Sunak announced a furlough scheme covering 80 per cent of employees' wages, up to £2,500 per month, to encourage employers to keep staff on as the crisis worsened. In a tacit admission that the current welfare system barely provides claimants with enough to survive, Sunak injected it with an extra £7 billion, equivalent to an extra £20 per week for the unemployed. But many of the UK's 5 million self-employed workers – including precarious workers in the gig economy – struggled to access a separate income-support scheme, while statutory sick pay remained at around £95 per week – one of the lowest rates of all advanced economies and not nearly enough for many people to pay their rent, let alone their bills, and basic living costs. In the US, meanwhile, Congress authorised a $1,200 one-time payment to every US adult: hardly enough to sustain 20 million unemployed American workers without health insurance and with uneven access to an opaque and ungenerous welfare system.[5]

There are differences between the crisis we are currently facing and the one that followed the financial meltdown of 2008. After 2008, many people lost their homes, and many more lost their jobs. The suffering was huge and not confined to the least well-off in society. But with the coronavirus recession, the economic risks are much more individualised and much more severe. With high rents, high transport costs and stagnant wages, the UK was already enduring a cost-of-living crisis before the coronavirus hit.[6] After a decade of government-imposed austerity, household savings were dangerously low, more than 8 million households struggling with some form of problem debt.[7] The year 2017 was the first since 1987 that households spent more than they earned, covering the difference by taking out new debt and drawing down from their savings.[8]

The furlough scheme, and the related support provided to the self-employed, alleviated some of the pain over the short term, but millions of people are struggling to make ends meet, and it won't take much to push them over the edge. The growing number of workers without stable employment face a continued substantial loss of work as businesses struggle to manage coronavirus-related restrictions, people reduce their consumption and public spaces have to shut down again periodically. Even if they manage to escape the virus, those without a stable income – self-employed people, those on zero-hours contracts and in the gig economy, plus freelancers, small business owners and those paid on commission – are in a tight spot.

For many states in the global South, meanwhile, the pandemic represents an existential threat. While these states were initially insulated from the spread of the virus, the caseload in peripheral areas of the global economy like sub-Saharan Africa is increasing. Many states already in debt distress before the pandemic began are now on the brink of default. Not enough support is being provided by international institutions and bilateral creditors to deal with the underlying problem: some states have too much debt ever to fully repay it. What support is being provided often comes with strings attached that simply deepen the relationships of dependency responsible for these problems in the first place. Governments are being forced to choose between honouring their obligations to creditors and providing the basic resources needed to fight the pandemic. The blatant and unjustified inequalities that continue to mark global capitalism will only deepen as climate breakdown decimates those states least responsible for its emergence.

How will the UK and other advanced capitalist states unwind from the emergency positions they have adopted? And how should such support be extended to the Global South? The optimal solution to the prolonged negative-demand shock from the coronavirus is a global Green New Deal: a huge package of state investment built around democratically decided public priorities, including the widening of democratic public ownership. Such a plan would both absorb the impact of the slowdown today and to improve the sustainability of the economy over the long term. States in core countries would undertake this investment themselves, while transferring technology and resources to governments in the Global South to allow them to do the same. New international development banks could also be created to support those states most at risk of extreme weather events, desertification and rising temperatures. A break with the rules and norms associated with the Washington Consensus could help to rebuild trust in international institutions and support a new era of fair and sustainable global cooperation.

While such a scenario might seem far-fetched, the costs of not acting would be extraordinarily high. The coronavirus crisis has provided the world with an insight into what life might look like as our environmental systems begin to collapse under the pressures of unending capitalist accumulation: a world ripped apart by a series of natural disasters, where many are unable to access the resources they need to survive, and strict limits must be imposed upon normal economic activity to prevent further deterioration of our natural systems.

Clearly, a continuation of lockdown is no solution to the problem of climate breakdown. The Great Lockdown did have an immediate impact on global emissions. However, this feat has been achieved through the extreme measure of bringing much economic activity to a near standstill. With many people unable to travel to work, and many more refraining from travelling and consuming in their usual ways, the human impact on the environment may be declining, but incomes are also constrained, supply chains interrupted, and millions are on the brink of poverty, homelessness and bankruptcy as a result.

Adaption to climate breakdown, and the recovery from the coronavirus, must be just – the costs, and potential benefits, must be distributed evenly, not imposed upon those least able to bear them. But if socialists seek to use this moment to argue for a transition to a green, sustainable economy – on the basis that climate breakdown presents a far more pressing existential challenge to humanity than the coronavirus over the long term – the Right will simply argue that such spending is unaffordable.

Even on a superficial level, this is false. A global Green New Deal of the kind that would allow advanced economies to reach net zero by 2030, giving the rest of the world more time to achieve their decarbonisation objectives, would entail huge levels of investment in green transport and energy infrastructure, research into green technologies and a substantial programme of green housebuilding and retrofitting. Such a programme would create jobs today, boosting demand, as well as expanding the amount the economy can produce over the long term, increasing tax revenues and therefore the creditworthiness of the states that participated.[9]

On a deeper level, the costs of failing to tackle climate breakdown are astronomical. Climate breakdown is accelerating at rates that would render many parts of the planet uninhabitable in just a few short years.[10] The past five years have been the warmest years since records began,[11] and the twenty warmest years have all occurred over the last twenty-two years.[12] With our forests being destroyed and our oceans acidified, it will not be long before we reach a series of tipping points when the effects of climate change will accelerate suddenly and unpredictably, rapidly creating the kind of 'hothouse earth' currently the stuff of science fiction.[13]

Even when assessed on purely economistic grounds, there is a clear case for wide-ranging intervention now to prevent longer-term damage to the economy and the environment. If we are to deal with climate change, trillions of dollars' worth of fossil fuels will have to stay in the ground, leaving fossil fuel companies with 'stranded assets'. When one accounts for this issue, equity valuations in the industry look extremely optimistic: some have argued the global economy is facing a carbon bubble worth between $1 trillion and $4 trillion.[14] If, on the other hand, those assets are retrieved, we'll be facing an overlapping environmental, political and economic catastrophe that will create trillions of dollars' worth of damage anyway. The question, then, isn't whether or not tackling climate change is affordable – it is who will pay for it.

Proponents of the Green New Deal are clear on this question: the wealthy are responsible for far more carbon emissions than the poor and should therefore bear a greater part of the burden of decarbonisation. According to Oxfam, the wealthiest 10 per cent of the global population is responsible for half of all emissions, and the top 10 per cent of the UK population is responsible for three times the level of domestic household emissions of the poorest 10 per cent.[15] Moreover, if we want to build mass support for decarbonisation, we must recognise and respond to the concerns of working people worried about the impact on jobs, transport and taxes.

Contrary to the insistence of many liberals, climate justice can only be brought about through systems change, not individual behavioural change. Polluters benefit from encouraging us to think about climate breakdown as an issue of individual responsibility: it would be very convenient for the oil companies if the public conversation around climate breakdown focused on plastic straws, recycling and veganism. The big polluters must be made to pay for the damage they have caused out of the profits they have generated. There is now evidence that the big polluters have known about the impact of burning fossil fuels since at least the 1970s, and yet they have earned billions of dollars' worth of profits since then – some of these even used to sponsor climate denialism.[16]

Instead of imposing carbon taxes, or encouraging small behavioural changes, working people must use their influence over state institutions to enforce constraints on polluting activities and promote investment to absorb job losses in carbon-intensive sectors. Focusing on recycling, energy-efficient light bulbs and plastic straws militates against the emergence of such a movement by encouraging people to think of climate breakdown in individualised terms. Equally, buzzwords like 'degrowth' conjure up images of scarcity and poverty that deter people from climate activism. Tackling climate breakdown requires a mass movement that can fight back against a capitalist system that exploits human beings as much as it does the natural environment.

The Green New Deal must be global – it must result from cooperation between working people, outside of existing international institutions. A global Green New Deal is not only necessary to combat the global threat of climate breakdown, but to tackle the regime of imperialism that underpins financial globalisation. Aside from helping to cause the 2008 financial crisis, capital mobility has sucked money out of the Global South and into financial vortexes such as Wall Street and the City of London. Now it is threatening the solvency of governments responsible for providing healthcare for billions of people in the midst of a global pandemic.

The first and most pressing priority must be a debt write-off for the Global South. Longer-term, the kind of state intervention required to tackle climate change – democratic public ownership over most of the economy, dramatic increases in state spending and the controls on capital mobility required to achieve this – are not merely frowned upon by the World Bank and the IMF, they are actively prohibited. Countries must unite to work on a new set of rules for the global economy. Different parts of the world must be able to choose their own routes to prosperity, rather than having neoliberalism foisted upon them. Powerful countries must end practices that actively harm the Global South. This crisis must lead to long-overdue reforms to international trade and investment law, which are required to tackle tax avoidance, promote innovation and prevent imperial extraction – and in the meantime, wealthy states must commit to undertaking direct resource and technology transfers to states in the Global South. And they must work with one another to combat climate change – based on the assumption that doing so will require levels of international coordination and public spending previously unseen during peacetime.

There is no guarantee that, instead of a Green New Deal, public opinion in the Global North will not endorse a return to austerity when the pandemic is over. To assume that after a period of largesse – a spending spree, a heavy drinking session – comes a period of atonement – a payback, a hangover – is embedded deep within our commonsense understanding of the world. These assumptions are strengthened by the lived experience of modern capitalism, which substitutes cheap credit for rising wages, only to create a mountain of unpayable private debt that hangs heavy over the heads of working people.

In the UK, the imperative for the governing Conservatives remains squaring the interests of their voter base with those of a highly internationalised and financialised capitalist class centred in the City of London; or, as Colin Leys puts it, how to 'resolve the tension between the requirements of global capital and the interests of the population whose votes they need to stay in power'.[17] There are some clear shared interests that unite all sections of British capital. A preference for light regulation and low corporate, income and wealth taxation (along with ways to avoid it) is one. Capital mobility is the foundation of the British economy's financialised and internationalised business model and is therefore another critical common interest of the British capitalist class. All sections of British capital require a strong British state capable of acting as a regulator and lender of last resort, an enforcer of contracts and a source of safe assets. The British state also provides direct avenues for profit seeking through, for example, procurement, outsourcing, consulting and accounting, and the privatisation of state assets, as well as acting to promote the interests of British capital abroad, generating foreign opportunities for accumulation.

Beyond this point, the picture is more mixed. The largest and best-organised portion of British capital, which consists of the largest businesses and financial institutions, is relatively unmoored from the British economy – the profits of these capitalists are not especially dependent upon the economic activities of British consumers, firms or the state – and it therefore has little interest in the state of British infrastructure, public services or wages. Other sections – notably, consumer-facing services and the remnants of British manufacturing – are more interested in these aspects of state spending. But the historic roots of the UK's financial, professional services and real estate sectors, along with their size and strong organisation, tend to mean that their interests dominate those of other sections of capital. This section of capital has every reason to prefer what Andrew Gamble called 'the free economy and the strong state': the British state must be strong enough to execute the wishes of capital at home and protect its interests abroad without closing off avenues to capital accumulation by expanding into activities that could be undertaken by the private sector.[18]

This is why the British state pursued austerity in the first place: it was a political rather than an economic imperative. Observers often take the aims of austerity at face value: to reduce the UK government deficit and the size of the national debt. They then look at the Conservative Party's austerity regime and read it as a failure: austerity collided with the global trend of secular stagnation to deliver a decade of low growth, low investment, stagnant wages and productivity, which compromised efforts to cut public debt and led to dramatic increases in private debt. But the British ruling class is not stupid – its members will undoubtedly have known that the best way to reduce the government debt would have been to invest and grow the British economy rather than to impose an austerity agenda that was always going to increase the relative weight of the government debt when compared to the national income. Austerity was never about reducing the deficit – it was about maintaining the political and economic power of the British ruling class at a time of deep fragility. It has never been more important for British capital to have control over the British state, given its importance to their accumulation strategies – and now basic survival.

Johnson and Sunak are under pressure from the Treasury and the City to undertake another fiscal clawback – what George Osborne terms 'a period of retrenchment and [of] trying to bring public sector debt down', to reassure bondholders.[19] But as policymakers should have learnt by now, swingeing cuts to state spending can actually exacerbate the scale of public debt relative to

GDP by curtailing output and causing further falls in tax revenues.[20] The government could attempt to boost receipts through some form of higher corporate taxation but unless it fails to tackle avoidance, this will not increase revenues by much. Wealth taxes are unacceptable given the demographics of the Tory voter base and the interests of British capital, while raising income tax, national insurance or VAT would impose more pressure on already strained incomes. Many workers will find themselves unemployed by the time the crisis is over, and a continued assault on workers' rights is one of the few ways the government can support profits without expanding the size of the state. Attempting to raise taxes on those who remain in work will not raise nearly enough revenue to account for the political pain.

At the same time, stabilising the Conservatives' electoral coalition will require Johnson to honour election promises to boost investment in the regions that delivered him his victory. Money for infrastructure investment will have to be found – though this investment will be undertaken under the auspices of the private sector, to ensure that the latter is not shut off from the benefits of government largesse. Spending on health and social care will also have to rise – though privatisation in these sectors is also likely to accelerate. The privatisation of other state-owned assets, however, pursued so rigorously by the last government, is paused as state-owned industries struggle in a harsher economic environment.

But a Green New Deal? Such an investment programme would provide limited support to long-time Conservative voters. Tory supporters – mainly older retired homeowners – have a clear set of common interests: house prices should remain high and their living standards protected. The creation of new, secure jobs and the increase in wages associated with the rising demand for labour would not benefit a largely retired electoral base. The majority either do not work or are about to retire so are unconcerned with jobs, wages, working time and labour rights. Their children are no longer in school, so they pay little attention to education policy and, being mostly well off, they are less concerned about areas of the welfare state outside of pensions, health and social care. Aware that climate change is unlikely to affect their living standards, they are generally less worried about environmental issues.

There are certainly some strong economic arguments for public investment to absorb the economic impact of the virus while also dealing with all the challenges that we faced before: mounting inequality, stagnant productivity and environmental breakdown. Implementing a significant package of state-led investment in the wake of this pandemic would, for example, have clear advantages for British capital: it would both provide direct avenues for profit seeking through state procurement, and de-risk investment in other sections of the economy by boosting employment, wages and therefore economic growth.

However, while there would undoubtedly be benefits for British manufacturers and consumer-facing services from a state-led decarbonising stimulus programme, the dominant highly internationalised and financialised sections of capital only need enough support from the state to survive, and a Green New Deal would bring with it difficult questions about the political determination of economic outcomes. In the long run, a global recovery is the thing that will sustain the profitability of British capital. At home, we may see a revival of some of the social democratic methods of economic management used in the post-war period. Much more likely, however, will be the emergence of a nationalist-corporatist model of economic management that combines limited state support to politically active sections of the electorate with handouts for the rich and powerful.

For the most part, socialists failed to use the political opening generated by the 2008 financial crisis to move beyond – or even substantially alter – capitalism. Nearly everywhere, the ruling class clung on to power – either by absorbing insurgent new movements into fragile coalition governments or transforming themselves from within, often by channelling the anti-systemic pressure generated by the crisis into nationalism and xenophobia, without threatening the economic status quo ex ante. Given the Left's failure to take advantage of the crisis of 2008, which, on the surface, appeared to confirm all the socialist suppositions about the inherent unsustain-ability of financialised capitalism, what hope do we have that our response to the coronavirus will be any better?

Socialists tend to be weighed down by the lessons of the past – so often, we find ourselves fighting the last war. History does not repeat itself – the response to this crisis will be very different to the response to 2008, at least in part because of the efforts of socialists to delegitimise neoliberalism and austerity – but it does rhyme. The costs of this crisis will, just like the costs of the last one, be felt most acutely by the most vulnerable in society.

Economic crises, and the market concentration and ruling class cooperation they engender, are not avoidable kinks in the system but an inherent feature of any version of capitalist accumulation: you cannot have capitalism without crisis, without centralisation or without cronyism. Inevitably, each successive adaption to crisis generates new fissures and contradictions, of which socialists can take advantage if we are sufficiently well-organised. One such fissure can be detected in the growing politicisation of economic activity.

The free market ideology which serves to legitimise forms of government intervention that support the interests of capital and prohibit state interventions that might increase the power of workers has been placed under significant strain in the period since the financial crisis. As we have seen, the foundation of this ideology is the separation between politics and economics.[21] For this ideology to retain its credibility, certain areas of economic policy must be naturalised and their distributive implications hidden to support the fiction that outcomes in these areas are the inevitable result of the operation of market forces – for example, the idea that there is a 'natural' rate of interest determined by the demand for and supply of money has been a powerful force for legitimating central bank independence and the technocratic determination of monetary policy.[22]

But retaining this distinction has become much harder in an era where state intervention is necessary to ensure the continued functioning of markets. When states are targeting asset prices, providing wholesale bailouts to private corporations and buying up substantial portions of their own debt, it becomes far harder to argue that interventions to promote the public good are undesirable because they might disrupt the operation of the market mechanism. Coordinated action to tackle poverty, inequality and climate breakdown becomes far harder to oppose in the context of an already-interventionist state. Indeed, this insight is part of what explains the authoritarianism of many interventionist states, which limit the demands that can be made on the state politically and legally rather than simply ideologically.

The expansion in the size of the state associated with the coronavirus outbreak has already triggered a certain amount of angst among many on the Left. Many are wondering what role socialism can possibly play in British politics now that the critique of austerity, which sat at the core of Corbynism, seems less relevant. In fact, this crisis is revealing the inherent weaknesses of the anti-austerity narrative that underpinned Corbynism. Socialism does not simply mean expanding the size of the capitalist state. Socialism means taking power away from the ruling classes – senior politicians, business owners and financiers – and handing it back to the people. In order to achieve this goal, it is not enough to demand a bigger state – the nature of the state, and of all our economic and political institutions, must be fundamentally transformed if we are to meet the challenge posed by economic stagnation, the pandemic and, perhaps most important of all, climate breakdown. Over the long term, the public must become engaged in the rational planning of economic activity – human beings must work together to determine democratically the best use of our collective resources.

There is a clear case not simply for state planning that prioritises the pursuit of equality, workers' rights and environmental sustainability, but for democratic public planning of economic activity. Before the pandemic, just 2 per cent of people thought the British economy wasn't in need of some degree of reform, while 63 per cent were in favour of a Green New Deal. The corona crash has undoubtedly seen public support for state intervention rise even further. A YouGov poll in April 2020 showed that 72 per cent of people supported the creation of a jobs guarantee scheme, 51 per cent supported a universal basic income 'where the government makes sure everyone has an income, without a means test or a requirement to work', and 74 per cent supported rent controls.[23]

The inefficiencies, inequities and corruption generated by state-monopoly capitalism do not result from centralisation in itself, but from centralisation absent the centrifugal force of democratic accountability. In the wake of this crisis, the resources by then under the command of the state should be allocated by the public, for the public. Absent the extension of the principles of political democracy into the realm of the economy, this crisis, like so many others, will simply be exploited by capital, for capital.

Notes

Preface

1 John M. Barry, 'The Single Most Important Lesson From the 1918 Influenza', *New York Times*, 17 March 2020.

2 Kim Moody, 'How "Just-in-Time" Capitalism Spread COVID-19', *Spectre*, 8 April 2020.

3 James Politi, 'Fed's Bullard Says Risk of Financial Crisis Remains', *Financial Times*, 2 June 2020.

4 Stephen Morris, George Parker and Daniel Thomas, 'UK Banks Warn 40%–50% of "Bounce Back" Borrowers Will Default', *Financial Times*, 31 May 2020.

5 OBR, *Fiscal sustainability report 2020*, Office for Budget Responsibility, 2020.

6 Sergei Klebnikov, 'How Bad Will Unemployment Get? Here's What the Experts Predict', *Forbes*, 31 March 2020.

7 Phillip Inman, 'UK Economy Likely to Suffer Worst Covid-19 Damage, Says OECD', *Guardian*, 10 June 2020.

8 International Labour Organization and Organisation for Economic Co-operation and Development, 'The Labour Share in G20 Economies', report prepared for the G20 Employment Working Group, Antalya, Turkey, 26–27 February 2015.

9 Shawn Donnan, 'Globalisation in Retreat: Capital

Flows Decline since Crisis', *Financial Times*, 21 August 2017; Susan Lund, Eckart Windhagen, James Manyika, Philipp Härle, Jonathan Woetzel and Diana Goldshtein, 'The New Dynamics of Financial Globalization', McKinsey Global Institute, August 2017.

10 Chibuike Oguh and Alexandre Tanzi, 'Global Debt of $244 Trillion Nears Record Despite Faster Growth', *Bloomberg*, 15 January 2019.

11 For a discussion of these forecasts, see Grace Blakeley, 'The Next Crash: Why the World Is Unprepared for the Economic Dangers Ahead', *New Statesman*, 6 March 2019.

12 Ibid.

13 Tithi Bhattacharya and Gareth Dale, 'Covid Capitalism: General tendencies and possible "leaps"', *Spectre*, 23 April 2020.

14 See IMF, *Policy Responses to Covid-19: Policy Tracker*, Washington, DC: International Monetary Fund, 2020.

15 In full, the Commercial Paper Funding Facility, Primary Market Corporate Credit Facility, Secondary Market Corporate Credit Facility, Term Asset-Backed Securities Loan Facility, Primary Dealer Credit Facility and Municipal Liquidity Facility.

16 Scott Minerd, 'We Are All Government-Sponsored Enterprises Now', *Global CIO Outlook*, Guggenheim Investments, 10 May 2020.

17 Philip Turner, 'Containing the Dollar Credit Crunch', Project Syndicate, 18 May 2020.

18 Robert Brenner, 'Escalating Plunder', *New Left Review* 123, May-June 2020, p. 22.

1 The Last Days of Finance Capitalism

1 BEA, 'GDP by State', Suitland, MD: US Bureau of Economic Analysis, 2020, bea.gov.

2 Drew DeSilver, 'For Most U.S. Workers, Real Wages

Have Barely Budged in Decades', Washington, DC: Pew Research Center, 7 August 2018.

3 BIS, 'Total Credit to Non-Financial Corporations (Core Debt) as a Percentage of GDP', Basel: Bank for International Settlements , 2020, stats.bis.org.

4 Chris Giles, 'Bank of England Drops Productivity Optimism and Lowers Expectations', *Financial Times*, 30 January 2020.

5 World Bank, 'Gross Fixed Capital Formation (% of GDP)', *World Bank Economic Policy & Debt: National Accounts: Shares of GDP & Other*, data.worldbank.org; Office for National Statistics, *UK Balance of Payments, The Pink Book: 2019*.

6 See, for example, FocusEconomics, '23 Economic Experts Weigh In: Why Is Productivity Growth So Low?', *FocusEconomics*, 20 April 2017.

7 Grace Blakeley, *Stolen: How to Save the World from Financialisation*, London: Repeater, 2019.

8 Andrew Haldane, 'The Contribution of the Financial Sector – Miracle or Mirage?', speech at the Future of Finance conference, London, 14 July 2010, bis.org.

9 Ibid.

10 Michael Hudson, *Killing the Host: How Financial Parasites and Debt Bondage Destroy the Global Economy*, Petrolia, CA: CounterPunch, 2015.

11 J.M. Keynes, *The General Theory of Employment, Interest and Money*, London: Macmillan, 1936.

12 Rudolf Hilferding, *Finance Capital: A Study of the Latest Phase of Capitalist Development*, ed. Tom Bottomore, London: Routledge & Kegan Paul, 1981 [1910].

13 Blakeley, *Stolen*, 'Chapter Two: Vulture Capitalism: The Financialisation of the Corporation'.

14 Thomas Philippon, 'The Economics and Politics of Market Concentration', *NBER Reporter*, no. 4, December 2019.

15 Karsten Kohler, Alexander Guschanski and Engelbert

Stockhammer, 'The Impact of Financialisation on the Wage Share: A Theoretical Clarification And Empirical Test', *Cambridge Journal of Economics* 43, no. 4 (July 2019).

16 Mimoza Shabani, Judith Tyson, Jan Toporowski and Terry McKinley, 'The Financial System in the UK', *FESSUD Studies in Financial Systems*, no. 14, February 2015.

17 Josh Ryan Collins, Laurie Macfarlane and Toby Lloyd, *Rethinking the Economics of Land and Housing*, London: Zed Books, 2017.

18 Blakeley, *Stolen*, 'Chapter Three: Let Them Eat Houses: The Financialisation of the Household'.

19 Colin Crouch, 'Privatised Keynesianism: An Unacknowledged Policy Regime', *British Journal of Politics and International Relations* 11, no. 3 (August 2009).

20 Adam Tooze, 'Notes on the Global Condition: Of Bond Vigilantes, Central Bankers and the Crisis, 2008–2017', 2017, adamtooze.com.

21 Zak Cope, *The Wealth of (Some) Nations: Imperialism and the Mechanics of Value Transfer*, London: Pluto, 2019.

22 Grace Blakeley, 'On Borrowed Time: Finance and the UK Current Account Deficit', Institute for Public Policy Research, Commission on Economic Justice, 2018.

23 Blakeley, *Stolen*, 'Chapter One: The Golden Age of Capitalism'.

24 Jeremy Green, 'Anglo-American Development, the Euromarkets, and the Deeper Origins of Neoliberal Deregulation', *Review of International Studies* 42, no. 3 (July 2016): 425–49.

25 Philip Mirowski and Dieter Plehwe, eds, *The Road from Mont Pelerin: The Making of the Neoliberal Thought Collective*, Cambridge, MA: Harvard University Press, 2009.

26 Grace Blakeley, 'On Borrowed Time'; Bank of England, 'North Sea Oil and Gas: Costs and Benefits', *Bank of*

England Quarterly Statistical Bulletin, March 1982.

27 Office for National Statistics, 'Changes in the Economy Since the 1970s', 2019, ons.gov.uk.

28 Cope, *The Wealth of (some) Nations.*

29 'Five facts about the UK service sector', Office for National Statistics, 29 September 2016.

30 Crouch, 'Privatised Keynesianism'.

31 ONS, 'Employees in the UK by Industry: 2018', Office for National Statistics, 26 September 2019, ons.gov.uk.

32 Blakeley, *Stolen.*

33 Richard Disney and Guannan Luo, 'The Right to Buy Public Housing in Britain: A Welfare Analysis', *Journal of Housing Economics* 35 (March 2017): 51–68.

34 Collins et al., *Rethinking the Economics of Land and Housing.*

35 Shabani et al., 'The Financial System in the UK'.

36 Ibid.

37 Ibid.

38 Thomas Hale, 'The Bank of England Has a Strange Idea of What QE Achieved', *Financial Times Alphaville*, 3 August 2018, ftalphaville.ft.com.

39 Jannes van Loon and Manuel B. Aalbers, 'How Real Estate Became "Just Another Asset Class": The Financialization of the Investment Strategies of Dutch Institutional Investors', *European Planning Studies* 25, no. 2 (February 2017): 221–40.

40 Adam Tooze, *Crashed: How a Decade of Financial Crises Changed the World*, New York: Penguin, 2018.

41 Jane Kelly, Julia Le Blanc and Reamonn Lydon, *Pockets of Risk in European Housing Markets: Then and Now, Working Paper 2277*, European Systemic Risk Board, 2019.

42 Adam Corlett, Arun Advani and Andy Summers, 'Who gains? The importance of accounting for capital gains', *Resolution Foundation*, 21 May 2020.

43 Carys Roberts, Grace Blakeley and Luke Murphy, *A Wealth of Difference: Reforming Wealth Taxation in the*

UK, Institute for Public Policy Research [IPPR], 2018.

44 Stephen Clark et al., *Are We Nearly There Yet? Spring Budget 2017 and the 15 Year Squeeze on Family and Public Finances*, London: Resolution Foundation, 2017, resolutionfoundation.org.

45 Josephine Cumbo and Robin Wigglesworth, ' "Their House Is on Fire": The Pensions Crisis Sweeping the World', *Financial Times*, 17 November 2019.

46 Richard C. Koo, *The Other Half of Macroeconomics and the Fate of Globalization*, Chichester, UK: Wiley, 2018.

47 Grace Blakeley, 'The Next Crash: Why the World Is Unprepared for the Economic Dangers Ahead', *New Statesman*, 6 March 2019.

48 Rana Foroohar, 'Tech Companies Are the New Investment Banks', *Financial Times*, 11 February 2018.

49 Koo, *The Other Half of Macroeconomics*.

50 Chibuike Oguh and Alexandre Tanzi, 'Global Debt of $244 Trillion Nears Record Despite Faster Growth', *Bloomberg*, 15 January 2020.

2 Into State Monopoly Capitalism

1 Philip Aldrick and Gurpreet Narwan, 'We'll Do Whatever It Takes, Central Banks Vow', *The Times*, 27 March 2020; Scott Minerd, 'Prepare for the Era of Recrimination', *Global CIO Outlook*, Guggenheim Investments, 26 April 2020.

2 Rudolf Hilferding, *Finance Capital: A Study of the Latest Phase of Capitalist Development*, ed. Tom Bottomore, London: Routledge & Kegan Paul, 1981, p. 234.

3 Karl Marx, *Capital: A Critique of Political Economy, Vol. 1*, trans. by Ben Fowkes, London: Penguin, 1990, pp. 777 and 929.

4 Hilferding, *Finance Capital*, p. 235; V. I. Lenin,

Imperialism, the Highest Stage of Capitalism, London: Lawrence & Wishart, 1988 [1917]; Paul A. Baran and Paul M. Sweezy, *Monopoly Capital: An Essay on the American Economic and Social Order*, New York: Monthly Review Press, 1966; John Bellamy Foster, 'Monopoly-Finance Capital', *Monthly Review*, vol. 58, no. 7, December 2006.

5 Ryan Banerjee and Boris Hofmann, 'The rise of zombie firms: causes and consequences', *Bank for International Settlements Quarterly Review*, September 2018.

6 Michalis Nikiforos, 'When Two Minskyan Processes Meet a Large Shock: The Economic Implications of the Pandemic', Levy Economics Institute, Policy Note 2020/1 (March 2020).

7 Martin Arnold and Brendan Greeley, 'Central Banks Stimulus Is Distorting Financial Markets, BIS Finds', *Financial Times*, 7 October 2019.

8 Jesse Colombo, 'The US Is Experiencing a Dangerous Corporate Debt Bubble', *Forbes*, 29 August 2018; Phillip Inman, 'Corporate Debt Could Be the Next Sub-Prime Crisis, Warns Banking Body', *Guardian*, 30 June 2019.

9 Matthew Watson, 'Re-establishing What Went Wrong Before: The Greenspan Put as Macroeconomic Modellers' New Normal', *Journal of Critical Globalisation Studies*, no. 7 (2014): 80–101.

10 Alfie Stirling, *Just about Managing Demand: Reforming the UK's Macroeconomic Policy Framework*, London: Institute for Public Policy Research [IPPR], 2018.

11 Marx, *Capital, Vol. 1*, p. 929.

12 Rana Foroohar, *Don't Be Evil: The Case Against Big Tech*, New York: Currency/Random House, 2019.

13 See, e.g., Jonathan Taplin, *Move Fast and Break Things: How Google, Facebook and Amazon Cornered Culture and Undermined Democracy*, New York: Little, Brown, 2017, in which the author makes the now well-known claim that 'Data is . . . the new oil'.

14 Foroohar, *Don't Be Evil*; Martin Wolf, 'Why Rigged Capitalism Is Damaging Liberal Democracy', *Financial Times*, 18 September 2019.

15 Foroohar, *Don't Be Evil*.

16 Matt Phillips, 'Investors Bet Giant Companies Will Dominate After Crisis', *New York Times*, 28 April 2020.

17 Matthew Vincent, 'Loss-Making Tech Companies Are Floating Like It's 1999', *Financial Times*, 16 June 2019.

18 Martin Wolf, 'Corporate Savings Are Contributing to the Savings Glut', *Financial Times*, 17 November 2015; Peter Chen, Loukas Karabarbounis and Brent Neiman, 'The Global Corporate Saving Glut: Long-Term Evidence', *VoxEU*, CEPR Policy Portal, 5 April 2017.

19 Rana Forooha, 'Tech Companies Are the New Investment Banks', *Financial Times*, 11 February 2018.

20 Andres Diaz, 'I'm a Small Business Owner. Where's My Coronavirus Bailout?', *Guardian*, 21 April 2020; Jonathan Tepper, 'Federal Reserve Has Encouraged Moral Hazard on a Grand Scale', *Financial Times*, 13 April 2020.

21 Robert Brenner, 'Escalating Plunder', *New Left Review* 123, May-June 2020, pp. 6-9.

22 Geoff Mann, *In the Long Run We Are All Dead: Keynesianism, Political Economy, and Revolution* London: Verso, 2017.

23 Ellen Meiksins Wood, *Democracy Against Capitalism: Renewing Historical Materialism,* London: Verso, 2016.

24 Gillian Tett, 'Why the US Federal Reserve Turned Again to Blackrock for Help', *Financial Times*, 26 March 2020; Michael Bird, 'European Central Bank Hires Blackrock to Help with Loan Purchase Programme', *City A.M.*, 27 August 2014, cityam.com.

3 The New Imperialism

1 Francis Fukuyama, 'The End of History?', *National Interest*, no. 16 (Summer 1989): 3–18, and *The End of History and the Last Man*, New York: Free Press, 1992; Thomas Friedman, *The World Is Flat: A Brief History of the Twenty-First Century*, New York: Farrar, Strauss, and Giroux, 2005.

2 Karl Marx, *Capital: A Critique of Political Economy, Vol. 1*, trans. by Ben Fowkes, London: Penguin, 1990, p. 450.

3 There is a long-standing debate in Marxist literature about the class position of the manager: see Nicos Poulantzas, *Classes in Contemporary Capitalism*, London: Verso, 1975; John Ehrenreich and Barbara Ehrenreich, 'The Professional-Managerial Class', in *Between Labour and Capital*, ed. Pat Barker, Boston: South End, 1979; Erik Olin Wright, *Classes*, London: Verso, 1985; Gérard Duménil and Dominique Lévy, *Managerial Capitalism: Ownership, Management and the Coming New Mode of Production*, London: Pluto, 2005.

4 Zak Cope, *The Wealth of (Some) Nations: Imperialism and the Mechanics of Value Transfer*, London: Pluto, 2019.

5 V.I. Lenin, *Imperialism, the Highest Stage of Capitalism*, London: Lawrence & Wishart, 1988 [1917].

6 Rudolf Hilferding, *Finance Capital: A Study of the Latest Phase of Capitalist Development*, ed. Tom Bottomore, London: Routledge & Kegan Paul 1981 [1910]; Lenin, *Imperialism*.

7 *Honest Accounts 2017: How the World Profits from Africa's Wealth*, Jubilee Debt Campaign, 2017, globaljustice.org.uk.

8 For a discussion of the impact of these strategies, see Cope, *The Wealth of (Some) Nations*; T.J. Coles, *Privatized Planet: Free Trade as a Weapon Against Democracy, Healthcare and the Environment*, Oxford: New Internationalist, 2019.

9 Cope, *Wealth of (Some) Nations.*

10 Jenny Chan, Mark Selden and Pun Ngai, *Dying for an iPhone: Apple, Foxconn, and The Lives of China's Workers*, London: Pluto, 2020.

11 Kwame Nkrumah, *Neo-Colonialism: The Last Stage of Imperialism*, London: Thomas Nelson, 1965, p. ix.

12 Many newly independent states were saddled with debts accrued by colonial administrations, with citizens forced to repay debts that had been used to subjugate them. Further on in the post-independence period, many repressive regimes accrued vast debts in order to consolidate their power (often with the support of the United States), which would then be passed on to democratically elected leaders once they had been deposed. These 'odious debts' are the subject of Léonce Ndikumana and James K. Boyce's *Africa's Odious Debts: How Foreign Loans and Capital Flight Bled a Continent*, London: Zed, 2011.

13 Michael Thomson, Alexander Kentikelenis and Thomas Stubbs, 'Structural Adjustment Programmes Adversely Affect Vulnerable Populations: A Systematic-Narrative Review of Their Effect on Child and Maternal Health', *Public Health Reviews* 38, no. 13, 2017.

14 UNCTAD, *The Least Developed Countries 2000 Report*, New York and Geneva: UNCTAD, 2000.

15 Gianluca Benigno, Luca Fornaro and Martin Wolf, 'The Global Financial Resource Curse', Federal Reserve Bank of New York Staff Report No. 915, February 2020.

16 Philip R. Lane, 'Financial Globalisation and the Crisis', BIS Working Paper 397, Basel: Bank for International Settlements, December 2012.

17 *Trade and Development Report, 2008: Commodity Prices, Capital Flows and the Financing of Investment*, New York and Geneva: UNCTAD, 2008.

18 Benigno, Fornaro and Wolf, 'Global Financial Resource Curse'.

19 Grace Blakeley, 'On Borrowed Time: Finance and the

UK Current Account Deficit', Institute for Public Policy Research, Commission on Economic Justice, 2018.

20 International Monetary Fund, 'Zambia: 2019 Article IV Consultation – Press Release', IMF Staff Report: Country Report No. 19/263, 2 August 2019; 'The World Bank In Zambia: Overview', World Bank, worldbank. org, last updated 13 October 2019.

21 'Zambia to Pay Vulture Fund $15.4m', *Lusaka Times*, 25 April 2007.

22 Twiwwe Siwale, 'The Structural Constraints Limiting Zambia's Economic Response to COVID-19', London: International Growth Centre, 22 April 2020.

23 Tayyab Mahmud, 'Is It Greek or Déjà Vu All Over Again?: Neoliberalism and Winners and Losers of International Debt Crises', *Loyola University Chicago Law Journal* 42, no. 4 (2011): 668–83; Adam Tooze, 'Notes on the Global Condition: Of Bond Vigilantes, Central Bankers and the Crisis, 2008–2017', adamtooze. com, 7 November 2017.

24 'Fears Grow over Bangladesh's COVID-19 Response', *Al Jazeera*, 23 March 2020.

25 Stephanie Kelton, *The Deficit Myth: Modern Monetary Theory and the Birth of the People's Economy*, New York: PublicAffairs/Perseus, 2020.

26 Mahir Binici and Mehmet Yörükoğlu, 'Capital Flows in the Post-Global Financial Crisis Era: Implications for Financial Stability and Monetary Policy', BIS Working Papers 57, Basel: Bank for International Settlements, 2015, 319–43.

27 Gabriel Chodorow-Reich, 'Effects of Unconventional Monetary Policy on Financial Institutions', Brookings Papers on Economic Activity, The Brookings Institution, vol. 48, no. 1 (Spring 2014): 155–227.

28 Martin Mühleisen and Mark Flanagan, 'Three Steps to Avert a Debt Crisis', *IMF Blog*, 18 January 2019, blogs. imf.org.

29 'The Great Lockdown: Worst Economic Downturn Since the Great Depression', IMF press release, no. 20/98, 23 March 2020.

30 Nick Dearden, 'The Global South's Coronavirus Debt Crisis', *Tribune*, 10 May 2020, tribunemag.co.uk.

31 Rehman Sobhan, 'Structural Maladjustment: Bangladesh's Experience with Market Reforms', *Economic and Political Weekly* 28, no. 19 (8 May 1993): 925–31.

32 Amy Kazmin, 'Modi the Reformer Reappears as Coronavirus Hits India's Economy', *Financial Times*, 15 May 2020.

33 See IMF, *Policy Responses to Covid-19: Policy Tracker*, Washington, DC: International Monetary Fund, 2020.

34 Ibid.

35 UNCTAD, *Digital Economy Report 2019: Value Creation and Capture: Implications for Developing Countries*, Geneva: United Nations Conference on Trade and Development, 2019.

36 A global debt jubilee was partially achieved in 2000, when the Jubilee Debt Coalition – a network of charities and religious organisations – pressured the UK government to write off a substantial portion of the debts owed to it by Global South states. Several other countries followed suit. But it was not long before these debts began to accrue once again.

37 See, for example, 'Coronavirus: Cancel the Debts of Countries in the Global South', Jubilee Debt Campaign, 18 March 2020, jubileedebt.org.uk.

38 Sarah-Jayne Clifton, 'Coronavirus Could Collapse the World's Poorest Economies', *Tribune*, 11 April 2020, tribunemag.co.uk.

4 Reconstruction

1 'Republicans Suddenly Find a Bailout They Can Back', *Politico*, 18 March 2020; 'Trump Pivots to "Phase Two", Risking More Death to Save Economy', *Bloomberg*, 6 May 2020.

2 Irving Fisher, *The Debt-Deflation Theory of Great Depressions*, Cleveland: Econometric Society, 1933.

3 CEIC Data, 'Private Consumption: % of GDP by Country Comparison', 2020, ceicdata.com.

4 Gary Stevenson, 'Following the Coronavirus Money Trail', *Open Democracy*, 27 March 2020.

5 Luke Savage, 'One Cheque Isn't Enough', *Jacobin*, 26 May 2020.

6 Richard Partington, 'Living Costs Rising Faster for UK's Poorest Families Than Richest', *Guardian*, 25 April 2019.

7 Claer Barrett, 'Inside the UK's Debt Crisis', *Financial Times*, 26 April 2019.

8 Richard Partington, 'UK Households Spend above Their Income for Longest Period Since 1980s', *Guardian*, 29 March 2019.

9 Ann Pettifor, *The Case for the Green New Deal*, London and New York: Verso, 2019.

10 David Wallace-Wells, *The Uninhabitable Earth: Life After Warming*, New York: Tim Duggan/Random House, 2020.

11 Alejandra Borunda, 'The Last Five Years Were the Hottest Ever, NASA and NOAA Declare', *National Geographic*, 9 April 2019, nationalgeographic.co.uk.

12 Laurie Laybourn-Langton, Lesley Rankin and Darren Baxter, *This Is a Crisis: Facing up to the Age of Environmental Breakdown*, London: Institute for Public Policy Research, 2019.

13 Will Steffen et al., 'Trajectories of the Earth System in the Anthropocene', PNAS August 2018, 115, no. 33: 8252–59, pnas.org.

14 Fiona Harvey, 'What Is the Carbon Bubble and What Will Happen if It Bursts?', *Guardian*, 4 June 2018.

15 Oxfam, 'World's Richest 10% Produce Half of Carbon Emissions While Poorest 3.5 Billion Account for Just a Tenth', Oxfam International press release, 2 December 2015, oxfam.org.

16 Shannon Hall, 'Exxon Knew about Climate Change

Almost 40 Years Ago', *Scientific American*, 26 October 2015.

17 Colin Leys, 'The British Ruling Class', in *Socialist Register 2014: Registering Class*, eds, Leo Panitch, Greg Albo and Vivek Chibber, London: Merlin Press, 2014, 108.

18 Andrew Gamble, *The Free Economy and the Strong State: The Politics of Thatcherism*, Basingstoke, UK: Palgrave, 1988.

19 Andrew Atkinson, 'George Osborne, Architect of UK Austerity, Says New Cuts Needed Post-Crisis', *Bloomberg*, 20 April 2020; 'Treasury Blueprint to Raise Taxes and Freeze Wages to Pay for £300bn Coronavirus Bill', *Telegraph*, 12 May 2020.

20 Jonathan Ostry, Prakash Loungani and Davide Furceri, 'Neoliberalism: Oversold?', *IMF Finance and Development* 53, no. 2 (June 2016), imf.org.

21 Ellen Meiksins Wood, *Democracy Against Capitalism: Renewing Historical Materialism*, London: Verso, 2016.

22 Peter Mair, *Ruling the Void: The Hollowing of Western Democracy*, London and New York: Verso, 2013.

23 IPPR, 'Public Support for a Paradigm Shift in Economic Policy', Institute for Public Policy Research, 17 November 2019, ippr.org; Labour for a Green New Deal, 'Majority of Public Support Ending Net Zero 2030 Emissions Target, Poll Finds', press release, 7 November 2019, labourgnd.uk; 'Public Support Universal Basic Income, Job Guarantee and Rent Controls to Respond to Coronavirus Pandemic, Poll Finds', *Independent*, 27 April 2020.